CUTE FRUIT

CUTE FRUIT

A 52-Week Devotional for You and Your Children on the Fruit of the Spirit

By Alexandra Schroder & Amy Winner

Illustrations by Aila Winner

Author photographs courtesy of Elisabeth Dorosh and Malina Funes

Published by Game Changer Publishing

Paperback ISBN: 979-8-90158-003-5

Hardcover ISBN: 979-8-90158-004-2

Digital ISBN: 979-8-90158-005-9

GAME CHANGER PUBLISHING

www.GameChangerPublishing.com

This book is dedicated to my sweet Jack and Emmy.
My prayer for you is that you will find your JOY in the Lord
and that you will always know your unique, incredible worth in Him.
I can't wait to see the amazing plans God has for you.
You are so special and so loved. :)
~AS

This book is dedicated to Andy.
You are my encouragement and favorite person. Thank you for being all in when I didn't know I could do it.

I also dedicate it to Aila and Archie.
I am your biggest fan, and it makes my heart full that you both chose ME instead of the shoes I was deciding between.

Also for Alex.
You are the best person I could have made this happen with.
My favorite teammate!!

And finally, I dedicate this to Jesus.
Through You, all things are possible!
~ AW

Advance Praise

"Leave it to a rainy day at Disney! Instead of feeling discouraged, Alex and Amy dreamed up this devotional for families—*Cute Fruit!*

Designed to guide families through the ordinary ups and downs of life with encouragement to take life's lemons and turn them into—not just lemonade but into something even *more* fruitful!?

Lemons into lemonade. Dreary days into divine ideas. Rain into rainbows. Alex and Amy, take our hands and guide us along your way and into the way of the Spirit!"

– Lisa Nichols Hickman,
Author of *Mercy and Melons: Praying the Alphabet*

"As a filmmaker, podcaster, preacher, and long-time worker, I wear many hats. Yet, in the middle of all my responsibilities, I must never lose sight of my greatest calling—my family. That is why *Cute Fruit* is so meaningful. This 52-week devotional gently reminds us to place God and family first, guiding our hearts before life can pull us in every direction. Each week provides a fresh opportunity to refocus, to draw closer to God, and to strengthen the bonds that matter most. May this devotional inspire you, as it has inspired me, to choose family first every day."

– David L. Walker,
Filmmaker, Writer, Editor, and Preacher;
Director of *Prayer* & *Prayer 2,* and other faith-based films

"What could be sweeter than parents and children growing together in their faith? *Cute Fruit* brings Scripture to life in a memorable way for the whole family. Each week includes thoughtful devotions for both parents and children, meaningful prayers, and simple, fun activities that draw families closer to God and one another. By pairing each virtue with a real fruit—like love with strawberries and joy with lemons—this devotional makes the Fruit of the Spirit both tangible and unforgettable. In a world where families are hungry for truth and togetherness, *Cute Fruit* serves up both in abundance."

– Amy Schneider, Co-Founder, Eyes of Faith

"As a family with kids ages 10 and 12, we've loved using this devotional together. The kids say it's different and fun, especially the engaging activities at the end of each lesson.

Each night before bed, we gather to read, pray, and grow together, applying the fruits of the Spirit in our daily lives. We love the thoughtful structure: the parent section provides helpful background, the family lesson draws us together around God's Word, and the guided prayer at the end helps us close with focus and connection.

I also know the authors personally, and they are radiant examples of Christ's love. One author, in particular, has been my best friend for many years and shines God's love through her family, her career, and her everyday life. It has been a joy to see God using her to spread His light through this devotional.

As a pastor and a therapist, we can confidently say this resource fosters spiritual growth while strengthening family connection. We're so grateful to have it in our home."

– The Dericks Family: Nicole, Founder of Clarity Counseling;
Rev. Chris Dericks, Pastor; and Norah & Nolan

"*Cute Fruit* beautifully blends biblical truth with practical activities that engage the whole family. Alex and Amy's unique gifts as teachers, mothers, and Christians shine through every page, providing tangible ways to live out the Fruits of the Spirit. As a parent, this is exactly the kind of resource I've been longing for and one I will return to again and again."

– Elisabeth Dorosh,
Small business owner, and Christian Mama of two littles

"Amy is a true testament to grace in action—an 'angel on earth' in the way she shows up, listens, and lifts people higher. She lives fully and loves deeply, and it shows in the way she encourages everyone around her.

She's my first call for tough questions about kids, marriage, career, or just life. Her advice is practical, and her joyful, God-centered faith always points me back to God. Her perspective is wise, kind, and steady.

A quick note about her family, too: From the moment I met Alex, Amy's sister-in-law, I noticed that same kind and accepting heart. She loved on my kids, and you could see how much she loves God in her life. That spirit runs through their whole family.

Cute Fruit is the perfect book for families to read and complete together. Because I know Amy's heart and how she shows up for people, I can recommend Amy—and anything she and Alex write—with full confidence."

– Ashley DeCoy,
Faithful Friend, Mom of Three, and Overcomer

"Alex and I met the summer before kindergarten, and along with many of our other friends, we tried to spend as much time together as we could until we graduated high school. The soccer field, the drama stage, the band performance, the pizza shop: We could have fun anywhere! When you interact with the same people in this many different arenas, you learn about their true character. Regardless of the atmosphere, I have noticed two consistent qualities in Alex. First, Alex has *always* been a wellspring of joy. Her laughter is the soundtrack to so many of our friends' memories; it is the love, joy, peace (and so forth) pouring out of her heart and into ours. Secondly, she is receptive. Alex is always listening more than she's talking, and she is always on the lookout for God's lessons. Every detail of life seems to nudge her toward faith in her Lord. Because she is the kindest soul, I am so thankful she has an annual audience of 5-year-olds in her kindergarten classroom. I can't think of a better influence. Now she is expanding that audience through this book, letting us all in on her softness of heart, and I know her entries will resonate with the families who read it.

I love the way Alex and Amy genuinely share their detailed snippets of their lives that remind us that God's Spirit works through the ordinary. Rather than taking on a tone of instruction, the authors write as companions to the reader, pulling back the curtain on their own experiences of learning to walk by the Spirit.

Their multi-faceted approach to writing makes *Cute Fruit* a devotional that you can adapt for whatever your day holds. If you have time for a sit-down lesson with the whole family, you have all the resources you need. If you're looking to pray for a particular Fruit of the Spirit, you have so many prayers at your fingertips. If you're wanting to make an abstract idea about godliness more tangible, 'Cute Fruit' has 52 suggested activities to help us understand these lessons in a hands-on way. I love the heart behind this book and its accessibility for families, and I can't wait to share a copy with my own kids!"

– MaryLou Dovan,
Lifelong Friend, Wife, Mother of Four

"What a wonderful Scripture-based and family-centered devotion resource! So many of the devotion materials we attempt to use in our busy lives are focused and designed to be done separately with individual family members only, such as devotions for parents, women, men, and children. *Cute Fruit* is a fresh devotional approach that is fun, relevant, and brings together an interactive and intergenerational experience for all family members using child-created illustrations and a 'spiritually healthy' devotional diet with 'Biblical Fruit' that all can enjoy together!"

– Rev. Douglas Winner

"From giggles to deep conversations, this devotional guides families to live out love, joy, peace, and all the Spirit's Fruit in everyday life. As an educator, I love resources that help kids learn in memorable ways—and this devotional does just that! Each lesson takes the Fruit of the Spirit off the page and plants it in children's hearts, helping families grow in love together."

– Leann Davis,
Educator at Beaver Area School District

"As 2 Corinthians 3:17 says, 'Now the Lord is the Spirit, and where the Spirit of the Lord is, there is freedom,' I highly recommend *Cute Fruit* for families, ministry leaders, and churches. After decades in ministry, it is a joy to endorse a devotional that unites families with faith, hope, and love. It is a unique book, as it combines the creativity and imagination of a child with truth found only in pure freedom in the Spirit of the Lord. *Cute Fruit* should be on the shelf of every home and church, as it confirms the promise of John 1:5: 'The light shines in the darkness, and the darkness has not overcome it.' May we all bear the *Cute Fruit* that our world needs in the name of Jesus."

– Amy Bordonaro,
Student and Family Ministries Director, Pastor,
Free Three Anti-Trafficking Executive Director

"This amazing family devotional is the nutrition we can all benefit from by 'tasting and seeing that the Lord is good.' What incredible reminders each devotion brings to draw us into a deeper relationship with our Creator and each other. We live in a fast-paced, digital, self-centered world where stopping to delight in God's word, promises, and instructions gets increasingly harder for families. I am excited to see how God continues to use *Cute Fruit* beyond this devotional! May the testimonies of its impact be shared for the Glory of God!"

– Bethany Wentz,
Executive Director, Dream Big Honduras

"As a mom striving to raise godly, wise children with strong character, *Cute Fruit* is exactly the type of family devotion we needed! The reflections are heartfelt and inviting, while the practical prayers and simple activities make it easy to live out biblical truths in everyday life. This book is not only engaging for kids of all ages, but it also draws the whole family closer to God. I can't recommend it highly enough—a must-buy and must-read for every Christian family!"

— Jaime Dray,
Mom of 3 & Business Owner

"We all need the daily reminder of how the Holy Spirit works in our lives. *Cute Fruit* unites the older and younger generations and provides the opportunity to share the love of Christ in all that we do!"

– Kimberly Walker,
Christian Dance Educator and Studio Owner,
Generation Dance Company

"*Cute Fruit* is the perfect devotional for busy families. It's more than a book; it's an invitation to build moments that matter together. Adding *Cute Fruit* to our morning routine encouraged a simple but meaningful pause—an intentional way to stop and connect with God and with each other. Instead of letting life rush past, *Cute Fruit* helps families make life special, memorable, and rooted in joy. Written by two people I deeply admire for the way they parent, spread joy, and live out their faith, it's both effortless and meaningful, creating a simple pause in the day to make life more thoughtful, special, and memorable together."

– Nicole Hunter,
Visionary, Irons Mill Farmstead;
Wife, mom, creative-curator

"*Cute Fruit* demonstrates how the Fruit of the Spirit is not just 'cute,' but is also significant in the values of a family and in the development of children.

Framed around thoughtful selections of Scripture, authors Alex and Amy shine a winsome light on the nine Spirit-inspired virtues the Apostle Paul brilliantly enumerated in his Epistle to the Galatians. They deftly incorporate personal anecdotes to illustrate how each of the Fruits can impact aspects of everyday life as the wonder and majesty of God is unveiled. The weekly segments will inspire intentionality through games to play, books to read, activities to pursue, and ideas to consider... all linked to one of the Fruits.

The next time you enjoy a juicy strawberry, or tantalize your taste buds with a savory peach, or enjoy a tiny blueberry, you might know the uncommon taste of the Fruit of the Spirit. Experience *Cute Fruit* and you will understand.

The prayer of *Cute Fruit* is that the Fruit of the Spirit might be emblazoned on the hearts and minds of the children and their families.

Cute Fruit is more an experience in which to engage than merely a book to read."

– Dr. Dar Huey,
Professor of Education at Westminster College,
Inspiring mentor to the authors in both
their professional and faith journeys

Read This First

It means a lot that you're reading our book.
Want to connect beyond the pages and keep growing with us?
We would love to have you join our Cute Fruit Family on Instagram (@cutefruitfamily), where you can follow us and be part of our community to grow together in the Fruit of the Spirit.

Scan the QR Code Here:

CUTE FRUIT

A 52-Week Devotional for You and Your Children on the Fruit of the Spirit

ALEXANDRA SCHRODER
AND AMY WINNER

Illustrated by Aila Winner

Foreword

I have been blessed to know one of the authors (Amy) since she was born and the other (Alex) since she was 10 years old. While they are, of course, unique individuals who are different in many ways, they also have quite a few similarities. They both love to read and write, exercise, travel (especially to the beach or Disney World!), eat ice cream, and spend time with their families. They are also both teachers, moms, daughters, sisters, and dog owners, as well as fun-loving and thoughtful women who have a heart for God and others.

Since Amy and Alex share so many similarities, it makes sense that they would also have a shared purpose for this book: to point families to Jesus. As a result, the hope is for parents and children to grow closer to Jesus as they grow closer to each other, while discovering more deeply the significance of the Fruit of the Spirit in their lives.

Here are a few important items to note about *Cute Fruit*:

1. ***It's all about Jesus.*** The main point of this devotional is to point families to JESUS—the One who loves each one of us enough to die for us. 1 John 4:9 (NLT) says, *"God showed how much He loved us by sending His one and only Son into the world so that we might have eternal life through Him."* God's great love is unconditional and unsurpassed. Without Jesus, we would all still be separated from God. Because Jesus died on the cross—conquering sin and death—and rose to life again, our relationship with God is restored. And when we turn from our sin, ask for forgiveness, and ask Jesus to come into our hearts, He promises us that He will. Not only that, but He also fills us with Himself—the Holy Spirit. Because of the love of the Father, the sacrifice of Jesus, and the gift of the Holy Spirit, we have access at any point to the Trinity. What an amazing God!
2. ***It's all about love.*** This devotional was created with the hope of sharing the love of God with others. When we try on our own to demonstrate the Fruit of the Spirit, our efforts can only take us so far. However, with the Holy Spirit inside us, God's love (and joy, peace, etc.) is shared freely. Our restored connection to God through Jesus allows God's love, not our own, to flow through us and reach out to touch those

around us. *Cute Fruit* gives countless opportunities for the seeds of love to be planted in each member of the family. Our prayer is that the Holy Spirit will "water" those seeds, and they will grow and bloom into even greater love that will be shared within (and beyond) each family. How truly incredible that God's love can be shared with and through those who believe!

3. ***It's all about families.*** Both Amy and Alex had a lot of support during the writing process of this devotional. Amy said, "Andy, Aila, and Archie have not only been the inspiration for many of the devotions written in this collection, but they've also been so helpful in trying out the different devotions and activities. They were happy to oblige as test subjects." Alex had just as much support from her family. She shared, "Josh, Jack, and Emmy have been the inspirations for a lot of the stories shared in this devotional. They have also been sounding boards and brainstormers and have helped test out activity ideas. Mostly, they have been wonderful encouragers through every step of the process." Nieces, nephews, and other extended family members have also played various roles in helping this devotional take shape. A few Christmases ago, our mom even "published" the first copy of *Cute Fruits* (which had been the working title at that point). That gesture meant so much to Amy and Alex and is just one example of how our families continue to show their love and support.

Cute Fruit is written by families, for families. Amy emphasized, "It's so important for us to share Jesus' love with our children, and the way we've set up this book allows us to explore it in a way that we can grow together as a family, as well as closer to Jesus." This devotional is meaningful for both kids and adults and encourages togetherness and family connection. There are memorable devotions and activities, simple and engaging discussion points, and purposeful Scripture verses. Additionally, extension activities provide a hands-on experience of the Fruit of the Spirit. What better way to spend time as a family than to connect with each other AND God?!

Cute Fruit is for everyone. May it be a blessing to you and your family as you spend time reading this devotional together. And as you flip through these pages, may laughter fill your home, Scripture shape your hearts, and the Holy Spirit grow fruit that will last.

May God bless you and your family, always, and fill you up with more and more of His love!

With love,
Melissa Dorosh
Amy's Sister & Alex's Sister-in-Law

Table of Contents

Introduction

"But the fruit of the Spirit is love, joy, peace, patience, kindness, goodness, faithfulness, gentleness, and self-control. Against such things there is no law."

– GALATIANS 5:22-23 (ESV)

A few years ago, we were sitting on a couple of inner tubes in our family's pool and talking about everything from highlights of a reality TV episode (our shared guilty pleasure!) to what was going on in our lives and what God was teaching us. We were with our nieces and nephews, and we started talking about our mutual love of writing, the Fruit of the Spirit, and what physical fruit we would envision each of the Fruit of the Spirit being. It was here that the idea for this devotional was born.

Since then, we have plugged away slowly but surely, some months writing a lot, while other months the shared Google doc collected some digital dust. Our lives also went through many changes, and our families evolved. Our world went through COVID, which you may hear us mention a few times in the devotions. Through it all, God's faithfulness has been evident, and He has revealed more about His character through teaching us about His love, joy, peace, patience, kindness, goodness, faithfulness, gentleness, and self-control.

The title *Cute Fruit* also came from one of our poolside brainstorm sessions years ago. We were inspired to come up with something appealing for family members of all ages to do together. As parents, we know our kids are drawn to things that are cute! So the title stuck, and we thought it was catchy. As we continued writing, however, we found the title to be somewhat of a misnomer: having the Fruit of the Spirit in our lives can be anything but cute! Yes, the cover art and fruit illustrations are cute. And things involving family time can be super cute (I'm sure your own children are adorable, right? We know ours are!). But the gift from God that is the Fruit of the Spirit is beyond powerful! So while "cute" might not be the word that resonates with the Fruit of the Spirit—especially after delving into some of the meatier conversations that come from this devotional—we are sticking with it... Because, you know, it's catchy, we like it, and we can call it what we want. So *Cute Fruit* it is! But feel free to call it "Powerful Fruit" or "Significant Fruit" or any other adjective that comes to mind if you prefer. We don't mind.

So now that we've covered that, moving right along! As busy parents, we have recognized that we are in desperate need of God's grace to bless us with His fruits. (As we reread this paragraph to proofread, we were literally interrupted at least six times!) Out of our own doing, we can quickly run dry, becoming short with our kids and not loving them in the way we hope. This journey has taught us more than ever how dependent we are on the Lord, each moment and every day, to be filled with His Spirit and to better care for those around us. It has been such a blessing to take the time to reflect and write, and we pray that it will be a blessing to you, too.

Now, for a few orders of business about what you can expect to find in this devotional! Each devotion in this book has five sections:

- **Scripture:** We have chosen verses from the New International Version of the Bible, unless otherwise noted.
- **Parents:** In this section, the adults can read through the devotion geared towards them. Some older children might also benefit from reading the content in this section.
- **Families:** The devotions here are geared toward children, but the whole family will enjoy reading them together.
- **Prayer:** After reading the Parents and Families devotions, pray together using the written prayer. Feel free to add your own specific prayers during this time as well.
- **Extension Activity:** At the end of each section, we have designated an activity that puts into practice the Fruit of the Spirit in each devotion. Some of these activities are more involved than others. If you need to make adjustments or have ideas that work better for your family, go for it! We are hoping our ideas inspire you and you can use them in whatever ways bring your family closer to God and to each other.

This book is separated into 52 different devotions. (We feel now is the appropriate time to note that there are 52 weeks in a year, as we're sure you're aware, in case that impacts how you approach reading this book.) Each section focuses on one Fruit of the Spirit at a time. So, for instance, you will read through all the "Love" devotions first, then all of the "Joy" ones, and so on. Additionally, many of the different Fruit of the Spirit characteristics beautifully overlap with each other and are interwoven in the Scripture verses; for example, a verse may mention multiple fruits, such as joy and peace. (If we find these circumstances where multiple Fruits of the Spirit were combined, we like to think of them as "Fruit Salad.") With there being 52 separate entries, this devotional is designed for families to savor and meditate on one devotion during the week. Take your time with the extension activities and pray throughout the week on how God can teach you more about that specific fruit. However, read and experience as you feel led! There may be some weeks where you go through multiple passages and others where you don't, and that's okay too! Like visiting with an old friend, we pray that you will pick back up right where you left off and trust that God will meet you exactly where you are. His timing is always perfect.

As you begin this journey, we want to emphasize, as our sister, Melissa, so eloquently put it, that the Fruit of the Spirit is not about working or striving on our own and living out of our own strength. We can try our best to be loving and patient, to show kindness and goodness, and to have self-control, but without God's work in our hearts, it falls short. When we spend time with God—praying, reading the Bible, meditating on Scripture, and just being still in His presence—He fills us up with His love, as well as all of the other Fruit. That allows the Holy Spirit to work in and through us, and we can demonstrate all the different characteristics of God because we are first filled with Him and His love. In other words, God is the only One who fills us up, and from there we overflow with the Fruit of the Spirit.

May all the glory be to God! Mr. Rogers said it best: "The space between our mouth and the people's ears, or eyes, who receive what we make—that is holy ground." We pray too that this holy space between us and these words would not be our own, but that God would speak through them to you.

With all the love, joy, peace, patience, kindness, goodness, faithfulness, gentleness, and self-control that come from God alone,

Amy and Alex

One more thing...

Before we get to the devotions, this page describes the edible fruit we "picked" (see what we did there?) to go with each Fruit of the Spirit and our reasons why.

Additionally, these are the nine Fruit of the Spirit terms we are using throughout our devotional. You may come across some synonyms for these words depending on the Bible translation you read. We have thought long and hard about which actual fruit—as in, the kinds that we eat—we wanted to choose to represent each of the individual Fruits of the Spirit listed in the Bible. We are sharing them with you here and will also give a quick reminder at the beginning of each section... because this might just be the most "cute" part of our otherwise very important and powerful fruit.

Love: We represent *Love* with a *Strawberry!* Why? Well, you might have noticed that strawberries are red and heart-shaped. What better way to show love in fruit form?

Joy: We have chosen a *Lemon* to represent *Joy.* Yellow is one of the happiest colors—sunshine, brightness, golden glowing light, and so on. Also, sometimes, to find joy in our lives, we have to take lemons and turn them into lemonade. So we think this metaphor that we can use with the lemon fruit represents joy pretty clearly!

Peace: We have selected a *Peach* to represent *Peace*. First of all, the spellings are very similar, which we, as teachers, find aesthetically pleasing. Also, the light orangish color and soft peach fuzz remind us that the peace we feel can be calming, relaxing, and gentle. Lastly, you have certainly seen a peace sign—think 70s vibes! The peace sign is rounded just like the peach we have chosen to represent this Fruit of the Spirit.

Patience: For *Patience,* we chose to use a *Watermelon*. We like to think that, as we patiently pick out watermelon seeds before taking a bite of the juicy fruit, we can be reminded that having patience in our lives can often yield sweet results.

Kindness: *Kindness* is represented in this book as a *Pineapple*. Being kind sometimes means standing up (nice and tall, like a pineapple does) to express kindness towards someone. We can also look at the pineapple and remember not to be prickly, like the pineapple's exterior, but instead to be sweet and kind like the fruit inside.

Goodness: Purple *Grapes* are the fruit we chose to represent *Goodness.* First of all, they both start with the letter "G," so that was a minor connection worth noting. More importantly, though, purple grapes are also the color of royalty. We are all princes and princesses of God, as Children of the King. We can do much good for the Kingdom of God—what could be "more good" than grapes?!

Faithfulness: For *Faithfulness,* we chose the smallest fruit of our bunch: the *Blueberry!* We read in the Bible that you can have faith the size of a mustard seed, so the smallness of the blueberry is a reminder that with just a little faith, God can do great things.

Gentleness: The fruit we chose to represent *Gentleness* is the *Banana.* The inside of a banana can be easily bruised or squished, even with the peel on it. This is a fitting reminder that we must have gentleness so as not to cause any damage with our words or actions toward others.

Self-Control: The final fruit we chose is a green *Apple* for *Self-Control.* We have chosen to use a green (not red!) apple, which can be very sour and challenging to swallow (like so many things in our lives that require self-control). Green can also represent envy, like the envy we may have towards people who demonstrate the self-control we desire. Lastly, many people associate the apple with the forbidden fruit that Adam and Eve ate in the Garden of Eden, so we can make plenty of self-control connections with their story in the Bible.

We represent *Love* with a *Strawberry!* Why? Well, you might have noticed that strawberries are red and heart-shaped. What better way to show love in fruit form?

Love

God formed you for a reason, and
His thoughts about you are endless.

Scripture

"For you created my inmost being;
you knit me together in my mother's womb. I praise you because
I am fearfully and wonderfully made; your works are wonderful,
I know that full well.

My frame was not hidden from you when I was made in the secret place,
when I was woven together in the depths of the earth.
Your eyes saw my unformed body; all the days ordained for me
were written in your book before one of them came to be.

How precious to me are your thoughts, God!
How vast is the sum of them!
Were I to count them, they would outnumber the grains of sand
when I awake, I am still with you."

– PSALM 139 VERSES 13-19

Parents

Every summer for as long as I can remember, my family has visited Ocean City, New Jersey, for a week-long vacation at the beach. Thanks to the sunrises more vibrant than any Crayola crayon color combo, the sound of crashing waves, the feel of sandy walks, and yes, the surplus of cheesy fiction books and ice cream cones, it is easy to get lost in the midst of it all. Whatever problems, stressors, or anxieties that seemed so big beforehand suddenly dissipate in the vast magnificence of it all. I always find myself humbled at how small things really are, as I stand before the large ocean in front of me.

In today's social media world, it is so easy to compare our ordinary day-to-day lives to others' edited, seemingly perfect ones. It is easy to think of ourselves as less when we contrast what we are (or are not) doing compared to those around us. Adding that to the daily routines of work, errands, or checking off boxes on color-coded to-do lists (Yes, color-coded everything brings me joy!), sometimes I forget that the small moments, too, are sacred. Sometimes I forget that God created me both fearfully and wonderfully and that all of the little events and interactions, which may seem small and insignificant, are actually the pages that add up to create the book that God wrote for each of us in advance. Every little moment is ordained by God with great love, for great love. You matter, and every little moment matters.

So if you're ever like me and have a moment of feeling small, or ill-equipped, or insignificant, or that everything seems too hard, too big, or too overwhelming, do yourself a favor and turn to Psalm 139. Let God's love song wash over you as you remember that you are a wonderful creation, created for an incredible purpose, by a loving God whose thoughts of you are too many to name. Swim deeply in that love, and then let it overflow to those around you.

Families

Whether it is in the sand table at school, at the park, or at the beach, it is so fun to dig and mold and form something new out of tiny pieces of sand. Have you ever grabbed a handful of sand and tried to count how many pieces there are? If so, you were probably counting for a really, really long time because in one handful, there can be over 10,000 particles of sand! That's more stars than our naked eyes can see in the sky! Isn't that so crazy?!

The Bible says that for as many grains of sand as there are on Earth, that is how many thoughts He thinks about you a day. That's a lot of times that you are on God's mind! God formed you and thinks that you are absolutely wonderful. Before you were born, He knew that He had a special story designed specifically for you. :) Know that you are incredibly loved by God, and even if you feel alone, you can trust and know that He is always thinking about you, more times than the grains of sand on a beach or stars in the sky.

Prayer

God, thank you so much that you made me "fearfully and wonderfully." Thank you that even when I may feel small, or alone, or afraid, I can remember that you love me and are always thinking about me. Help me to live confidently in that love and share it with others. Amen.

Extension Activity

Play with some sand at the park, at home, or on the beach (and if you live by the beach—you're so lucky, and that's awesome!). Try to count how many pieces of sand are in your hand when you scoop up a handful. While playing, reflect on how much God loves you and that He is always thinking about you. Just like you can build creations that are unique and wonderful in the sandbox, God built you and those around you as a wonderful creation as well. Tell each other something that you love about how God created them.

Love

God's love is pure and challenges us to love without bounds when He is our Source.

Scripture

"Love is patient, love is kind. It does not envy, it does not boast, it is not proud. It does not dishonor others, it is not self-seeking, it is not easily angered, it keeps no record of wrongs. Love does not delight in evil but rejoices with the truth. It always protects, always trusts, always hopes, always perseveres. Love never fails."

– 1 CORINTHIANS 13:4-7

Parents

It is a snowy February day, and we just passed Valentine's Day! Although my husband thinks it is not an actual holiday—but rather one that was invented by greeting card and candy companies trying to make some extra money—I absolutely love it. What better excuse to celebrate love with the people you love?! This year I celebrated with family and friends watching the cheesiest rom-coms, making (and eating) yummy desserts, and getting my first facial (what better excuse to treat yo-self, as Rhetta from *Parks and Rec* says! And if you haven't had one before—WOW! Call and schedule one now!), and celebrated with my fourth-grade students by having a pajama and movie day at school. For any occasion presenting itself where the only requirements are to eat chocolate and watch chick flicks, I will be on board 110%, every single time.

Throughout my husband's and my dating relationship, there have been many moments and memories vivid in my mind. One of those was when he told me he loved me. I could tell that he was super nervous. He had something he had to tell me right away. I began to get nervous too—what was he about to say?! After pulling out his Bible (okay—that's a good sign!) with shaking hands, he said that when he was thinking of love, he went to Scripture to see what true love was. He then read to me 1 Corinthians 13. I can never hear that beautiful passage from Scripture now without thinking of that memory with Josh.

Reading through the Bible, you will find that Scripture is filled with words, proclamations, and definitions of the most radical love to ever be found on this planet—in this universe! Although the whole Bible is God's love letter to us, this passage in 1 Corinthians is one of my favorites because it exemplifies God's pure, unfathomable love. If we are blessed on Earth with glimpses and tiny examples of heavenly love through our relationships, then that is the greatest gift in the world. But no love on earth is perfect; no love on earth even measures close to the love of your Father, whose love is patient, kind, protective, and filled with hope. God's love never fails.

I encourage you today to open your Bible. Quiet yourself in the presence of your heavenly Father. Let His affirmations of love and what He thinks about you fill and soak into your soul. You are so loved by a perfect love, which your soul was created to find its rest in. Rest in His love today.

Families

Does your church have a Kids' Club or Youth Group? Maybe you've been to Sunday School or Vacation Bible School before? Growing up, those were some of my favorite communities to be a part of! I always loved the special activities and time with my friends.

During youth group one night, my pastor read to us 1 Corinthians 13. Go ahead and pull out your Bible and read it together now!

After we read through the passage, our pastor then challenged us to partner up with a friend. We were prompted to read 1 Corinthians 13, verses 4–7, to each other. However, any time that we saw the word "love," we were to substitute it with our partner's name instead.

In the Extension Activity below, you will be challenged to do this same activity! I hope that it will be as powerful for you as it was for me. It was amazing to hear those words spoken over me and to know that that is what true love is!

So often, the way I love gets twisted or manipulated by wavering feelings, tiredness, or even being annoyed! However, thankfully, we do not have to rely on ourselves to love each other. In fact, we can't love others well on our own. God loves you so much, and with His help, we can love others in this 1 Corinthians way too. Let God fill you and define you with His perfect love.

Prayer

God, thank you for your perfect love! Love that is patient, kind, pure, selfless, true, protective, trusting, hopeful, persevering, and flawless. Fill me with your love that I may share that incredible love with those around me. Let me learn about your great love more and more, that I may be refined and defined by it. Amen.

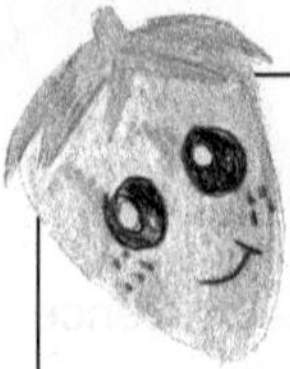

Extension Activity

Read the passage below! Anytime you see a blank line, say the name of your family member instead. Repeat until every name has been inserted into the passage.

How did it make you feel to hear your name? What did it make you think? How did it challenge you? What part stood out to you the most? Share what you think with one another.

__________ is patient, __________ is kind. __________ does not envy, __________ does not boast, __________ is not proud. __________ does not dishonor others, __________ is not self-seeking, __________ is not easily angered, __________ keeps no record of wrongs. __________ does not delight in evil but rejoices with the truth. __________ always protects, always trusts, always hopes, always perseveres.

Love

You are loved, not for what you do or how you perform, but for who you are and who you were created to be.

Scripture

"Yet you, Lord, are our Father.
We are the clay, you are the potter;
we are all the work of your hand."

– ISAIAH 64:8

"There is no fear in love. But perfect love drives out fear, because fear has to do with punishment. The one who fears is not made perfect in love."

– 1 JOHN 4:18

Parents

I remember once when I was ten years old, I was asked to sing a small solo during a song for our Christmas Eve church service. For weeks, I practiced, and you would have thought I was preparing to sing at a Taylor Swift concert in front of a million fans. It was the smallest solo, but I was so scared of messing up that when it came time to actually sing at church, they had to turn my microphone up to the highest volume to even hear a hint of my voice. To be honest, I'm not sure if anyone could hear anything! I was paralyzed by a fear of failure.

As I grew older, that same fear existed. I felt fine singing with a group in musicals, in choir, or at church. But when I was the only one singing and my voice was heard by others, my fear would take over. I was so worried about how I would sound or what would happen if I was off-pitch that I couldn't sing. My joy of singing was replaced by a paralyzing fear of messing up.

Singing wasn't the only area where I was affected by a fear of failure. This same fear consumed me on the soccer field, in relationships, and in the classroom. I felt as though my worth depended on how well I succeeded or did not succeed at something.

While in college, I had the opportunity to go to Malawi, Africa. This trip was a life-changing experience that allowed me to experience God's love in so many new and powerful ways. While staying with my host family, it came out that I sang at church, and when I replied that I knew how to sing "Amazing Grace," they instantly signed me up to sing in front of their congregation at church the next day. I was to sing the verses in English, and their daughter was going to sing them in Chichewa, the native language of Malawi.

Now, we're not talking about singing to a small, twenty-five-person church. Oh no. We're talking about hundreds of people! Did we practice beforehand? No! Had they ever even heard my voice before? No!

Something was different, though. Whereas life in America is fast-paced, filled with self-help books and busy schedules striving to make us the best and most productive beings on Earth, life in Malawi was the opposite. Time was different—it wasn't rushed and was all about relationships and being with people, even if that meant being late to events or even work. It was less about doing and performing and more about being and resting in who you were.

Singing at church in Africa is such a vivid memory in my heart because it was one of the only times, ever, where I wasn't motivated by the quality of my performance or fear of failure but was instead motivated by a heart of worship and praising God. As I sang, my voice wasn't coming from a place of desire to please others and succeed, but rather to bring glory to the One who created me. I was singing out of love rather than a place of fear. I felt right. I felt alive. I felt free.

Sometimes it is easy to think that our worth and value are dependent on our performance. If we are successful, we equate that to being good and okay and worthy of love, but if we fail, we can easily diminish our worth and value. The beautiful thing about God and our faith is that His love towards us is not dependent on the rising and falling of our performance. We are loved for who we are and who He created us (and is creating us and molding us) to be. All He wants is our hearts—hearts postured by worship, awe, and love for Him. All He wants is for us to keep showing up, leaning into Him and His Word, trying, and living out of love rather than fear. He loves us simply for who we are, not for what we do. Rest in that freedom today.

Families

Have you ever tried working with clay to make pottery before? Maybe molding a cup or a pot?

In art class when I was in middle school, we had the task of making a vase out of clay. Looking in shops at all of the perfect, smooth, flawless vases, I thought this would be a fun and easy project. Although it was fun, it was certainly not easy! It didn't matter how much I smoothed the wet, cool clay with my hands or worked with it over and over again; it would not get any less lumpy. My vision of a smooth and polished pot became that of a bumpy, lumpy, uneven pot of clay.

I had planned to give the vase to my mom for Mother's Day, but after seeing the final project, I wasn't so sure. What would she think? Where would she even want to display it, other than the back of our storage closet?

However, when I gave my mom the vase, all she saw was a beautiful masterpiece. The bumps and lumps and uneven sections didn't matter! What mattered was that I thought of her, tried my best, and gave her what I had. Twenty years later, it is still displayed in our house today.

The same is true with God. It doesn't matter the mistakes we made or our imperfect, bumpy, and lumpy parts. He loves us for the beautiful creation He has made us to be. Just like how we can mold clay into the shape and purpose we desire, we are clay in God's hands. In His eyes, we are perfectly and wonderfully made. There is no flaw in His beautiful creation, which is YOU! You are not defined by your lumps, bumps, or imperfect parts. You are defined by your loving God, who made you in His image—a beautiful creation for beautiful purposes.

Prayer

God, thank you so much for the gift of your Son. Thank you for the assurance and the knowledge that we are so loved by you. Even when we mess up, you still love us and remind us that we are not defined by our successes or failures. There is nothing we can do to earn more of your love, or anything we can do that would separate us from your love. When our hearts doubt our worth, remind us of your great love towards us. In Jesus' name, Amen.

Extension Activity

Borrow, buy, or find the book *Trying* by Kobi Yamada. A read-aloud version may even be on YouTube!

It is an amazing story about how we are not defined by our failures or even our successes. We are defined by our bravery in trying, showing up, and letting ourselves be molded and used along the way.

After reading the story, share with each other places where a fear of failure or messing up is holding you back from being who God created you to be. How can you encourage each other to step boldly into who you are in Christ?

Love

Who you are has a specific role to play in God's kingdom. Know that you are loved for your role, and strive to love and appreciate others for theirs.

Scripture

One Body but Many Parts

"Just as a body, though one, has many parts, but all its many parts form one body, so it is with Christ. For we were all baptized by one Spirit so as to form one body—whether Jews or Gentiles, slave or free—and we were all given the one Spirit to drink. Even so, the body is not made up of one part but of many.

Now if the foot should say, 'Because I am not a hand, I do not belong to the body,' it would not for that reason stop being part of the body. And if the ear should say, 'Because I am not an eye, I do not belong to the body,' it would not for that reason stop being part of the body. If the whole body were an eye, where would the sense of hearing be? If the whole body were an ear, where would the sense of smell be? But in fact God has placed the parts in the body, every one of them, just as he wanted them to be. If they were all one part, where would the body be? As it is, there are many parts but one body.

The eye cannot say to the hand, 'I don't need you!' And the head cannot say to the feet, 'I don't need you!' On the contrary, those parts of the body that seem to be weaker are indispensable, and the parts that we think are less honorable, we treat with special honor. And the parts that are unpresentable are treated with special modesty, while our presentable parts need no special treatment. But God has put the body together, giving greater honor to the parts that lacked it, so that there should be no division in the body, but that its parts should have equal concern for each other. If one part suffers, every part suffers with it; if one part is honored, every part rejoices with it.

Now you are the body of Christ, and each one of you is a part of it."

1 CORINTHIANS 12:12–27

Parents

When I first started teaching, I remember looking around at the other teachers around me. Wow—they were so good at what they did! Some were so strict and got students' attention by yelling. I have a pretty quiet voice, but maybe I should be louder and bolder? Yelling felt unnatural, but since others got command in their classroom that way, maybe I should too. Oh wow—look at that teacher! She uses this system to encourage her students to behave. What was I thinking about, handling it the way I was?! As I looked around me, I remember thinking about everyone else and how what they taught was so impressive. How could I possibly measure up?

So often I found myself comparing my gifts and talents to those around me. When someone is "more" of something in a room, it is easy to discount our gifts and talents entirely. We forget how God uniquely wired us as we compare ourselves to others.

I remember going on a run a couple of years later with a teacher who had actually taught me in second grade. I was still comparing who I was and trying other people's techniques, and I shared with her how the woman I had replaced was such a great teacher, and I felt like I could never be her. I will never forget her sharing with me that I have to teach exactly as I am. The only way for me to be effective with my students is to be me. Sure, we can learn from others and glean from their experiences, but we should never try to "be" them. Each of us has a part to play, and we can each reach different students based on our personalities and skill sets. If we all taught the same way, there could be a whole group of students unreached!

This passage is such a great reminder that each part of the body matters. You were designed exactly as you are to contribute to God's kingdom in a very specific way. We found out that we are expecting our first baby in November, and a friend recently said to me that our baby is uniquely handpicked for us, and we will be the best parents for that baby. I have been thinking a lot about that. I know that God has been and will be equipping us to be the parents this little girl or boy needs us to be! He will use the "body part" that we are, with its specific role and gift, to be a conduit of His love in the way that He designed us to.

So, the next time you are feeling inadequate, not enough, or that your role isn't valuable in comparison to others, remember this Scripture passage from 1 Corinthians. You are needed as you are, how you are. You are never too much of something or never not enough of something. Embrace the beautiful creation God has made you to be, and He will use you in incredible ways!

Families

Have you ever played on a sports team or watched a game on TV? If so, what is your favorite sport?

Now, for that sport, think of all of the positions on the field. My favorite sport is soccer, so I am going to use that as my example. On the soccer field, there are a goalkeeper, defenders, midfielders, and forwards. Every part is so important! If the team were all goalies, you wouldn't score any points. If everyone played forward, your team would give up a lot of goals! Every position on the team matters and plays a very important role.

Just like a position on a sports team, you have gifts that God has given you that are specific and unique, unlike anyone else. You were designed with purpose, for a purpose that only you can fulfill. There is no one like you. Know that you have an important role to play in the Body of Christ. God has a plan for creating you just the way He did: we are all one-of-a-kind individuals and have special gifts for a reason. Be proud of the amazing creation God has made you to be and celebrate each other's unique beauty.

Prayer

Dear God, thank you for your amazing creativity! Thank you for making so many different people in this world with so many different gifts. Thank you that no two people are the same. Thank you for making me, specifically, and for the gifts that you have given me. Help me today to use my gifts in a way that blesses others and honors you. In Jesus' name, Amen.

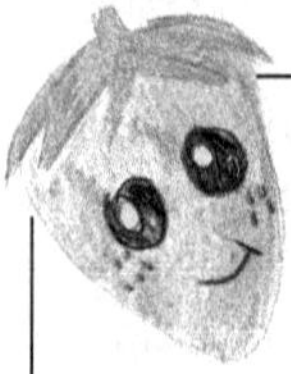

Extension Activity

Find a puzzle to do together. Our family loves Disney puzzles, but choose one that makes you happy, or whichever one you have at home! Look at all of the puzzle pieces individually. Notice how each one is so different, and by itself, we can't tell what the big picture is going to be!

After you are finished, notice how each piece is important. If one piece is missing, is the puzzle complete? Just like a puzzle piece, you are special and unique. Without you, your family is not complete, your classroom is not complete, your sports team is not complete, and your community is not complete! You have a very important role to play.

Love

God's love for us is deeper than
we can fathom.

Scripture

"For I am convinced that neither death nor life, neither angels nor demons, neither the present nor the future, nor any powers, neither height nor depth, nor anything else in all creation, will be able to separate us from the love of God that is in Christ Jesus our Lord."

– ROMANS 8:38-39

"And my God will meet all your needs according to the riches of his glory in Christ Jesus."

– PHILIPPIANS 4:19

Parents

When I was newly married, I was in a serious car crash. Somehow, I walked away with minor scrapes and serious whiplash, but my car was totaled. As was the semi-truck I had collided with.

This accident happened on a very short on-ramp as I entered the highway on the very first day of my new teaching job. My home at that time was about 3 miles away from where I was, and I called my husband, Andy, in hysterics to let him know what happened.

Then the emergency vehicles came, and the traffic jam I'd caused worsened. I felt so overwhelmed and lost. My car was an accordion of metal, and the semi (or were there two semis? It was all a blur...) was in bad shape. People and vehicles were swarming around the chaos I'd created.

Time seemed to stand still, swirling around me like a bad dream. That's when my hero, Andy, rolled up on his bicycle. (I learned later that the police officer who was manning the on-ramp briefly reprimanded him for biking onto a major highway, before Andy told him that his wife was the one in the accident. Then the officer kindly told him to get to me in the ambulance as soon as possible and that he would take care of getting his bike back to him. God bless that man and his kindness in that moment.)

If I'd been in my right mind, I might have been confused about how and why Andy had gotten there. But my knight in shining armor appeared at the scene of one of the worst possible moments, and he made it better just by being there for me.

Some days, love is found in the small moments. That day, though, I experienced love in a very big way. Andy didn't think about the "how" or "why" of it—he just knew he had to get to me, no matter what. (Kind of similar to God's pursuit of us, don't you think?)

How great is the love of my husband, who showed up for me in a major way when I needed him most. This is a reminder of the way that God shows up for us—in any way He knows we need Him to be there for us, like the verse from Philippians above reminds us.

Families

My family goes to a wonderful amusement park every summer—Idlewild Park and Soak Zone. I've gone there my whole life, and it was so special for me and my siblings to take our own children there so they could create their own special memories. My kids and their cousins have been going to Idlewild for as long as they can remember, which has been practically every summer of their lives.

When my daughter, Aila, was about three years old, she won a prize at the Idlewild duck pond: a stuffed animal popcorn! (Well, not a stuffed *animal,* but you know what I mean.) She was so happy... until her popcorn toy somehow made it to the other side of a wooden fence that she wasn't able or allowed to cross.

She was so heartbroken to lose her special new prize! She cried, and cried, and cried... until her big cousin, Max, came to the rescue! Max, who would have been about seven at that time, crawled to the other side of the fence to rescue the stuffed popcorn toy. Immediately, Aila's devastation was replaced by awe and gratitude for her big cousin.

To this day, when someone asks Aila who her hero is, she tells them it's her cousin, Max, because he rescued her popcorn. (And Aila is now older than Max would have been when this happened, but he will forever be her hero!)

Max didn't need to think hard about what he had to do to help his cousin. It probably wasn't even a big deal for him, but he returned Aila's popcorn toy to her because it was a way for him to be loving toward her. Max knew what Aila needed to feel loved and cared for, and he took care of her.

Similarly, as we read above in the verse from Philippians, we have a God who knows exactly what we need. The things in our lives—whether they're big or small—can't separate us from God's love for us. God's love is always offered to us in the ways we need it most. In fact, the biggest offering of God's love is His Son. The gift of Jesus is the greatest gift God could give!

Prayer

Lord God, to say that we are so grateful to you for your love doesn't even begin to express how meaningful your love is. You know what we need before we even need it, before we even ask you for it. Thank you for loving us in all the big ways and all the small ways and during all the moments of our lives. Help us to remember that nothing can separate us from your wonderful and glorious love. In your holy name, Amen.

Extension Activity

The Heart of a Hero: Think of a time someone was a hero in your life. Maybe it was for something small (like when you dropped your toy and someone helped you get it). Maybe it was something big (like when you were in a car crash and someone came to your rescue). Write them a letter or draw them a picture to say, "Thank you for having the Heart of a Hero!" and tell them exactly what they mean to you. Super bonus challenge: Try to find those little moments around you where *you* can step in and come to someone's rescue, and maybe even be their hero, in any big or small way!

Love

Simply because you exist, you are loved.
You are a child of God.

Scripture

"See what kind of love the Father has given to us, that we should be called children of God, and so we are."

– 1 JOHN 3:1

"For God so loved the world that he gave his one and only Son, that whoever believes in him shall not perish but have eternal life."

– JOHN 3:16

Parents

This past year, I gave birth to our first son, Jack. We truly felt God's presence with us throughout the day, in all the details, people present, and ways God orchestrated the timing for Jack's arrival into the world.

While we were pregnant with Jack, we chose to be surprised and not find out the gender. We thought **for sure** that he was a girl, but to our surprise, we were shocked to find out that he was a boy!

I will never forget the nurses placing Jack on my chest for the first time and looking into his sweet, big, dark eyes. I loved seeing his perfect little 7-pound, 1-oz body and ten long fingers and tiny toes. He was absolutely perfect, just the way he was. He was so loved, just the way he was. I couldn't believe how much I loved this sweet boy as soon as I met him. He didn't have to act a certain way for me to love him or do anything—I loved him so much, simply because he was my son. I loved him so much, simply because he was Jack.

Now, almost ten months later, I feel the same way! I am in total awe of who he is and who he is becoming. Every little thing he does and the way he grows is incredible and miraculous. There is nothing that he could do or couldn't do that would affect the depth of love I feel towards him.

My husband and I were just talking about how inconceivable it is that our Heavenly Father feels the same way about us, but infinitely more! We can't imagine loving anything as much as we love Jack, and God loves you, too, without limits. He loves us simply because we're Alex, or Amy, or Jack. He loves you simply because you're you. He loves everything about you and desires a relationship with you. Nothing you could do could add or detract from His love for you.

As John 3:16 tells us, *"For God so loved the world that He gave His one and only Son, that whoever believes in Him shall not perish but have eternal life."* What greater love is possible for us to imagine?! If you have already prayed the prayer of salvation, we are so thankful that you have accepted Jesus as your Savior. If you haven't already accepted Jesus into your heart, we urge you to pray the prayer below to know that you have accepted His sacrifice and Jesus as your savior.

So today, live knowing you are loved. So, so loved. And when you look at the sweet children entrusted to you, remember the first time you laid eyes on them—eyes filled with love, awe, and wonder. And know that your Father in heaven looks at you the same way.

Families

I don't know about you, but I **love** a good bubble bath. I love reading books and lighting a candle and just relaxing in the bathtub.

My son, Jack, also **loves** bath time. His time isn't quite as relaxing, though. He loves to play and splash and get water **everywhere!**

Whether you're a Jack or an Alex, bath time can be a lot of fun. But one time, it got pretty messy! I had a few things I needed to do, so I thought I would do my errands around the house while the tub was filling. It was a great idea—until I got distracted and caught up in a task and totally forgot about the bathtub. Water was everywhere. If you've seen the movie *Paddington* and the scene where he overflows the tub, it was like that (but maybe a little less extreme).

Just like the water that came out of the tub, God's love for you also overflows. It can't be contained by a tub, or a jar, or the biggest swimming pool or the largest ocean. His love for you is limitless. God loves you so much, exactly how you are!

Prayer

God, thank you so much for loving us so wholly and fully and perfectly. Thank you for being our Father, and for calling us your children. Draw us back to you today, reminding us how loved we are. Let your love fill us up and overflow into the lives around us today. In Jesus' name, Amen.

Prayer of Salvation

Lord Jesus, today I also say a special prayer for my salvation. I ask you to forgive me of all my sins. Jesus, come into my heart as my Lord and Savior! I surrender my life to you. I believe that you died on the cross for my sins and rose again to set me free from my sins. Be in my heart and fill me with your Holy Spirit. In your holy name I pray, Amen.

Extension Activity

Grab a cup and put it in the sink. Around the cup, put little bowls or containers so that they touch the glass in the middle. Turn on the faucet and let the water in the glass fill up. Once it fills up, watch how it spills out into the other containers surrounding it.

Think about how God's love fills you up. How does it feel inside knowing that you are loved by God? Talk about what it might look like for God's love to overflow and impact the people around you.

Joy

We have chosen the *Lemon* to represent *Joy*. Yellow is one of the happiest colors—sunshine, brightness, golden glowing light, and so on. Also, sometimes, to find joy in our lives, we have to take lemons and turn them into lemonade. So we think this metaphor that we can use with the lemon fruit represents joy pretty clearly!

Joy

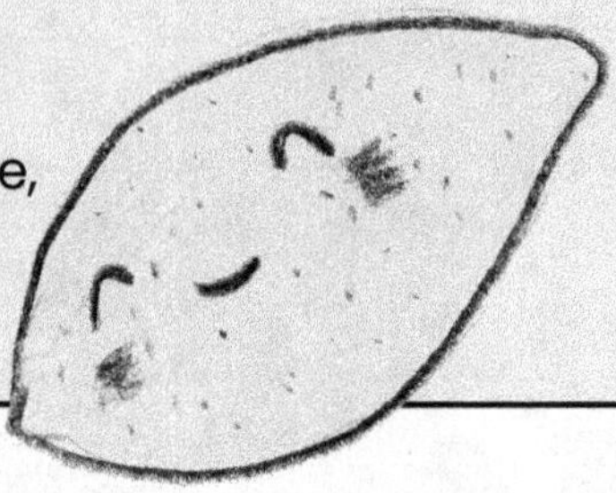

No matter what our circumstances are,
God has gifted us with a **joy** that
is found only in Him.

Scripture

"I rejoiced greatly in the Lord that at last you renewed your concern for me. Indeed, you were concerned, but you had no opportunity to show it. I am not saying this because I am in need, for I have learned to be content whatever the circumstances. I know what it is to be in need, and I know what it is to have plenty. I have learned the secret of being content in any and every situation, whether well fed or hungry, whether living in plenty or in want. I can do all this through him who gives me strength."

– PHILIPPIANS 4:10–13

Parents

A few years ago I had the opportunity to travel to Malawi, Africa. Malawi is a small country along the eastern coast of Africa. Although one of the poorest countries in the world with many families living below the poverty line, Malawi's motto is the "warm heart of Africa," and I found that description to be very accurate.

Throughout my time there, I saw remote villages lacking running water and electricity, and many people living without resources that you and I cannot imagine going a day without. However, I also saw the purest form of joy that I have ever witnessed. Despite lacking "essential" physical items, the Malawians gave what they had to us, prepared meals, invited us into their homes, and welcomed us with all that they were and with all that they had.

When I read this passage, I am reminded of my time in Africa. It's so easy to be swayed emotionally by happiness, sadness, and stress. For example, when I get a pumpkin spice latte, I am happy, but when I feel overwhelmed with schoolwork, the very next second, I feel inundated with stress. Circumstances are constantly evolving, good and bad things happen, and feelings come and go by the second. However, we do not have to live as victims or be captive to our ever-changing thoughts or emotions. Praise God that nothing can steal the joy He has given us. Even when we are going through trials, our hope and our joy can be found in Christ alone and the promise of eternity when we give our lives to Him.

Paul wrote this Scripture from Philippians while imprisoned, yet spoke with conviction that no matter our circumstances, we can tap into the joy God has given us. Just like the Malawians, our days are not dependent on our happiness, changing with our circumstances. Let us seek Him for our joy, having faith that no matter what happens in our days, we have a loving God who cares for us. As Ecclesiastes 3:11 says, *"He has made everything beautiful in its time."*

Families

What are some things that make you happy? Maybe it's going out for ice cream, listening and dancing to your favorite song, or having a playdate with a friend.

Now think about things that make you sad. Maybe you thought of a time that you fell and got hurt, lost something or someone you love, or when a friend said words that hurt your feelings.

God has gifted us with a lot of different feelings, and that's a great thing! A very special gift He gave us, though, is **joy**. Having joy means that we can always find joy in God, no matter what emotions we experience, happiness, sadness, or any other emotion that may change from one minute to the next. Living with joy means that no matter what happens to us, or no matter where we are, or what we are going through, we can have hope in our hearts, knowing that God is with us, loves us, and is working all things together for our good.

Prayer

God, thank you so much for your gift of joy. Thank you for all of the good things in life that make us happy. :) Thank you also for the reassurance that you are still with us when we are sad. Help us remember that we can find our constant joy in you, knowing that even when things don't go well or when we're sad, we can go to you for our comfort and joy. Amen.

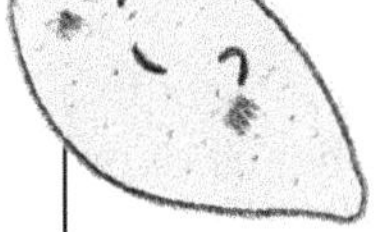

Extension Activity

Have a movie night with your family and watch *Inside Out*. Afterwards, talk about the different emotions that were in the movie that you may have felt. What stands out to you about joy?

Now think about how God has put joy in our hearts. How can we remember, especially during times when we are unhappy, that we can find **joy** and hope in God? Brainstorm some ideas with your family and try to do one together! (Examples could be writing out encouraging Scripture verses on sticky notes and putting them throughout your home, singing a song to brighten your spirits, or going to a special place when you're sad for quiet time to listen to music/draw a picture.)

Joy

Look for joy in the places you may not expect to find it.

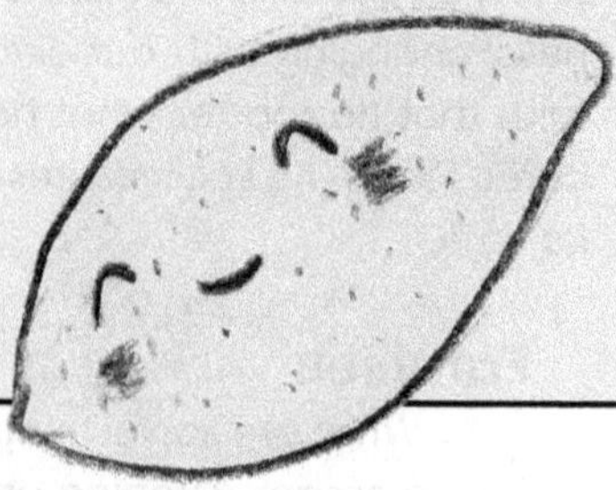

Scripture

"Consider it pure joy, my brothers and sisters, whenever you face trials of many kinds, because you know that the testing of your faith produces perseverance."

– JAMES 1:2-3

Parents

When I was in college, I was a resident assistant, and my good friend, Beth, was my resident director. At every staff meeting, Beth asked that we all share our "Roses and Thorns." Whatever was a blessing or something positive in our life could be shared as our Rose. Our Thorns would be something that went wrong or something that was bothering us.

This little activity allowed us to take a closer look at the joys and concerns in our lives, and often the small act of sharing our concerns would somehow turn that negative piece of our lives into something less negative; maybe not an outright joy per se, but it definitely put more of a positive spin on something bad.

Somehow, the act of opening up and talking about the concerns that bothered us so much actually enabled us to take ownership of those things and move on. It was, honestly, a very therapeutic process, and I realized the value of it so much that I continue doing "Roses and Thorns" with my own husband and children all these years later.

Most days, after my husband, Andy, and I get back from work and our two children get home from school, we take a minute to ask each other what our Roses and Thorns were from that day. This simple act has given each of us an opportunity to speak to the joys we are celebrating. It also gives us a safe space to share the worries that may be bringing us down. How often might we have glazed over our concerns, just because we didn't make a place where we could share them with each other? Just as importantly, how many moments might we have taken for granted without acknowledging them as celebrations and joys by naming them as our Roses?

We may often think of "joy" as exclusive to those happy, content, "rosy" things and moments in our lives. However, as the Scripture above reminds us, the trials and negative "thorny" moments in life can result in the perseverance that gives us the "pure joy" that can only come from God.

Families

Every day in our lives, we can name something good that happens to us or around us. Most days, we can also identify something that is bothering or worrying us. In my family, we call these our "Roses and Thorns."

My family regularly takes some time to share what our Roses and Thorns were from that day. The kids will share the good and bad parts of their day at school or something else that is important in their life at that moment. The grownups will do the same. We take time to listen to each other, celebrate each other, support each other, and encourage each other.

If we look very closely, we will see lots of Roses every single day, in almost every single moment! If you can find these good things and moments, congratulations! Your heart is open to the joy God gives us. From the smallest thing—like the song of a bird in springtime—to much bigger things—like a surprise visit from a favorite person or an unexpected gift—God's "Roses" of joy are all around us.

The difficult moments or circumstances—those thorny Thorns!—can be a challenge for us to deal with. The Scripture above tells us that, despite the trials and bad things in our lives that we may go through, we can have something called perseverance. Perseverance means to push yourself to work through the challenges you may face. When we go through the Thorns in our lives, this passage reminds us that those trials can give us perseverance. And even though it may not make the Thorn any better, it reminds us that God is using the challenges in our lives to give us perseverance.

God knows we experience Roses and Thorns every day. He celebrates with us when we thank Him for the joys and blessings He has given us! He is also there for us through the trials and difficult moments we endure.

Prayer

Heavenly Father, we thank you for the Roses in our lives. We are surrounded by your blessings in so many ways. We ask you to open our eyes to see these blessings in the big and small moments. We thank you, also, for the thorns we have to go through. We ask that you teach us perseverance when those difficulties challenge us and that we can receive the "pure joy" that only you can give us. It's in your name we pray, Amen.

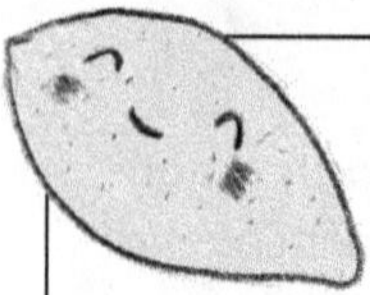

Extension Activity

If there was ever an obvious Extension Activity in this devotional, here it is! You guessed it: You're going to share your own Roses and Thorns with your family. Take turns sharing the Roses and Thorns from your day. It can be something big or small, or anywhere in between.

As your other family members share their Roses and Thorns, ask them questions about their responses. Encourage and celebrate each other's successes and joys. Offer support and a listening ear to the challenges and difficulties.

Why not make Roses and Thorns part of your daily routine? I recommend trying to find *together-time* to share these with your family. Dinnertime or bedtime might make the most sense, but your unique family can decide what works best for you. Enjoy learning a little bit more about each other as days pass, and ask for God's joy in all you experience in your lives.

Joy

Let your cup overflow with
the Joy of the Lord!

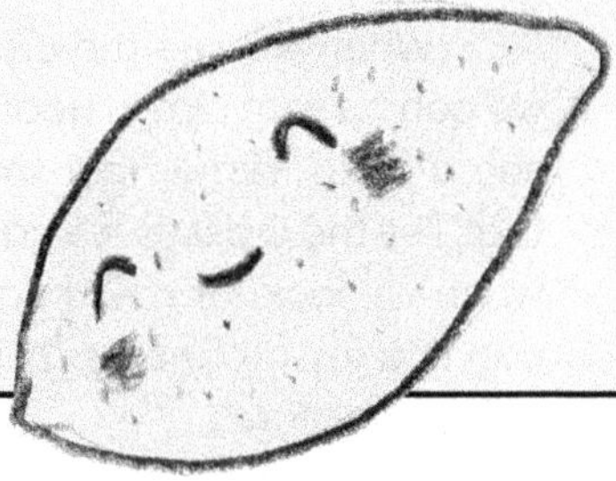

Scripture

"May the God of hope fill you with all joy and peace as you trust in him, so that you may overflow with hope by the power of the Holy Spirit."

– ROMANS 15:13

Parents

On a recent family vacation to Lake Erie, I was walking through the streets of the quiet town where we were staying. A small collection of sticks caught my eye, particularly two twigs that crisscrossed in a perfect cross formation.

As I continued my walk, I kept noticing little (seemingly unintentional) crosses everywhere: where the sidewalk cracks met. The fence posts. Tree branches. Windowpanes. So many crosses!

The cross is a beautiful reminder of the gift of salvation that Jesus gave us. Many people (myself included) wear a cross as a necklace or carry a cross with them as a visual reminder of this gift.

As I reflected on the crosses all around me, it reminded me of the joy that also exists all around me. Jesus dying on the cross means I can find joy in knowing I can be with him in Heaven someday!

No matter if it's the best day of my life or the worst (or more than likely, one of those in-between days), there is always *something* to be joyful for! Like the crosses I could find everywhere when I looked for them, joy is something I can also find everywhere when I look for it.

Families

My nephew's name is Max. When he was younger, he spelled his name "M-A-Cross." As a Christian family, we all thought this was really cute! We also knew it was great that he made connections to seeing the cross, even if it was a bit sideways in his name.

If we look closely, we can see crosses everywhere! Sure, maybe you see a cross at church, or on someone's necklace, or maybe in your home. But you can also see a cross if you look at things a little more closely: the stitching on the couch cushions. Wrinkles in our palms (or maybe elsewhere if we're a bit older...). Pencils or crayons in a bin. Branches in a tree.

When we see the cross, it is a reminder that Jesus died for us so we can be with him in Heaven someday. This is joyful news! Anytime you see a cross, remember that Jesus is with you always. Also remember that, like the crosses we can find if we look for them, we can also find joy when we look for it. We can find joy in Jesus being with us always; we can find joy around us all the time because there is always something to be joyful for.

Prayer

Dear God, thank you for sending us your Son to die on the cross, so we can have the promise of Heaven with you someday. Help us to remember the joy we have in your promise. Help us to look for joy all around us, and to be reminded of that joy anytime we see the cross. In your holy name we pray, Amen.

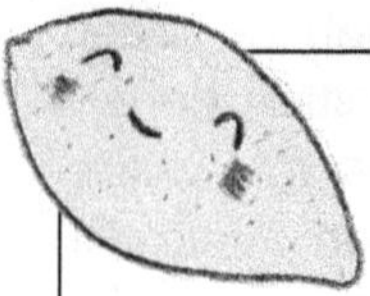

Extension Activity

Let's go on a cross-search together! You may decide to go for a walk or hike, or maybe just look around your own home. Try to find crosses anywhere you can. You may have to "look at the world from a different angle" (as my daughter Aila just told me), but you'll be able to see crosses everywhere if you look for them!

As I sit here writing, I see quite a few of them that I will share with you:

- Pattern in the placemats
- Wrought iron table legs
- Kitchen cupboards
- Toaster handle (okay, yes, I'm in my kitchen if you couldn't tell)
- Stair posts
- Chair backs

I could go on and on, and I haven't even moved (except my typing fingers, of course!).

While you find your crosses, remember that you can also find joy all around you. For each cross, try to name something you are joyful for! Here is a list I came up with off the top of my head to go with my cross list above:

- My loving family (even the one poking my back at this exact moment...)
- My home
- Music
- The sunshine
- Clothing (even though I have tons of laundry waiting for me to put away after I finish writing this, I'm grateful to have those clothes!)
- A fridge full of food (yep, still in my kitchen!)

This activity can happen today, but it can be an ongoing activity that you do whenever you see a cross, whether hidden or obvious. As you start to notice all the crosses all around you, try to also name the things that you are joyful for. There is always an opportunity to be joyful, and the reasons are countless!

Joy

Let no one take away your joy.

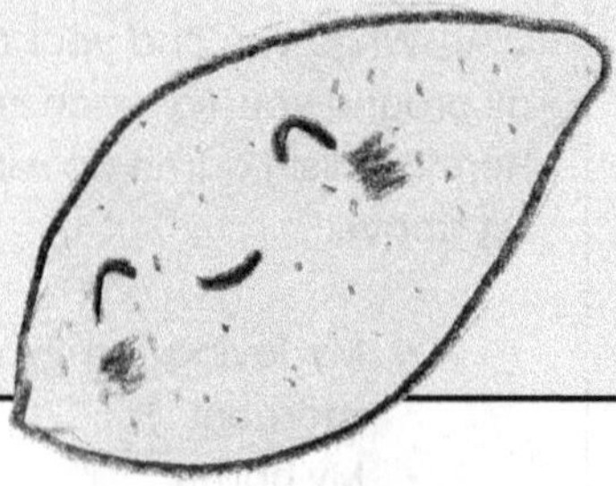

Scripture

"Very truly I tell you, you will weep and mourn while the world rejoices. You will grieve, but your grief will turn to joy. A woman giving birth to a child has pain because her time has come, but when her baby is born, she forgets the anguish because of her joy that a child is born into the world. So with you: Now is your time of grief, but I will see you again, and you will rejoice, and no one will take away your joy. In that day, you will no longer ask me anything. Very truly I tell you, my Father will give you whatever you ask in my name. Until now, you have not asked for anything in my name. Ask and you will receive, and your joy will be complete."

– JOHN 16:20–24

Parents

In the school where I teach, a parent and child became separated during a meet-the-teacher event. This poor parent was so distraught about not being able to find the child, and understandably so. We had security plans in place for making sure the students were safe, but the student was missing nonetheless.

The teachers and staff rallied together, and the child was found safe and sound but in the wrong classroom. As it turned out, there was a mix-up about which teacher the student had for the upcoming school year. English was their family's second language, and something was lost in translation when the child came back into the unfamiliar building after an outdoor recess. The parents' relief when they were reunited was palpable. What had been grief and despair moments before became joy and relief.

This story of grief-turned-to-joy reminds me of the Bible passage above, which describes a conversation Jesus had with His disciples shortly before He died on the cross. He knew they would feel grief and sadness, but that ultimately, because of His sacrifice and the miracle of His resurrection, they would experience joy. Even in those moments when we feel pain, sadness, or grief, we can remember the joy that is given to us through Jesus' sacrifice for our lives. There is truly nothing more significant than His promise to us that He died for our sins so we can live with Him eternally someday!

Families

Have you ever been to a place or country where they speak a different language than you do? Maybe you've even overheard people in your own community talking in a language you don't know.

When I was in college, I went to Italy with a group of choir students and professors to tour the country and sing in different Italian venues. I was fortunate that I traveled with a group of people from my college who could work together to figure out translations for most things. I know Spanish, and my understanding of Spanish helped (there are some similarities between the two languages). We also had Italian-English dictionaries and translators, or people who knew English, with us for most of our trip.

There were a few circumstances, however, when I couldn't understand what was being communicated, and I couldn't use my useful tricks to help me figure it out. I did my best to work through it, but sometimes things just ended up lost in translation.

What didn't get lost in translation, however, was a smile. When I couldn't communicate with someone, sometimes I got frustrated and upset. But one time, I remember an Italian person (whom I struggled to communicate with) gave me a big smile. No, I still have no clue what she was trying to say. But I smiled back, and we went on our way. I felt better, and my grief became joy because of that small act of the smile she offered me.

Whenever you feel upset, confused, or bothered by someone, why don't you try to give them a smile? Maybe that will help you both feel joy about something.

In the Bible passage above, Jesus told his disciples, his followers, that they would be very sad, but after that, they would be very happy. The disciples didn't know it yet, but Jesus was talking about when He would die on the cross. He knew that would make his followers very sad. But He also knew that they would celebrate and be filled with joy when He rose again, giving them the chance to live with Him forever in Heaven. Jesus has made this promise to you, too. What a joyful thing this is to all of us who accept Him into our hearts!

Prayer

Heavenly Father, thank you so much for the joy that comes in knowing that you have given us your Son so we can be with you for all eternity. Help us remember that we can find joy in you, even after we experience sadness, confusion, or grief. Thank you for always being with us, no matter what we are feeling. In Jesus' name we pray, Amen.

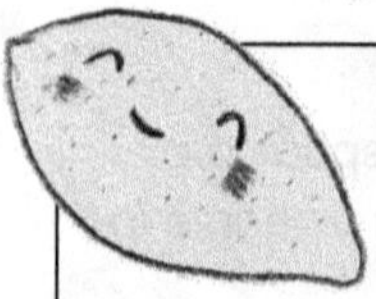

Extension Activity

Smile! You're spreading joy today! This challenge is easy: anyone you see today, give them a joyful smile! :-) You might make eye contact with someone at school, at a music or sports practice, at the store, or even at your home. When you do, give them a smile. You never know who needs a little joy sprinkled into their life today! (And, who knows? Maybe it'll make you feel pretty joyful, too!)

Joy

Give to the Lord as much as you can.

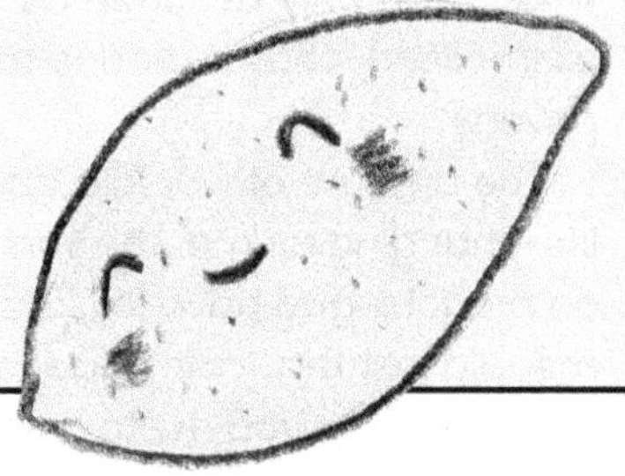

Scripture

"In the midst of a very severe trial, their overflowing joy and their extreme poverty welled up in rich generosity. For I testify that they gave as much as they were able, and even beyond their ability. Entirely on their own, they urgently pleaded with us for the privilege of sharing in this service to the Lord's people. And they exceeded our expectations: They gave themselves first of all to the Lord, and then by the will of God also to us."

– 2 CORINTHIANS 8:2–5

"Convinced of this, I know that I will remain, and I will continue with all of you for your progress and joy in the faith, so that through my being with you again your boasting in Christ Jesus will abound on account of me."

– PHILIPPIANS 1:25–26

Parents

When I was in high school, I had the opportunity to go on an international mission trip to Jamaica. Our church sent a team of mostly high school students and adults to do mission work with some underprivileged, impoverished Jamaicans. We were tasked with building several small, one-room homes for some families in need and also leading a Bible school for young children and families.

Prior to leaving for this trip, I was so motivated to share Jesus' love with all the Jamaicans we met! I wanted to give everything I possibly could to them—time, money, love, etc.—knowing I was coming from a place that had many things they didn't have.

After arriving and seeing firsthand the impoverished communities we would be serving, I gave myself a mental pat on the back for coming and "helping" them. However, God had something else in mind for me. Yes, our team had brought resources to share with the Jamaicans, but it turned out that the Jamaicans were the ones who ended up helping me.

As I began to build relationships with the Jamaican families, I was humbled by how much joy they demonstrated, despite their poverty. Here I was, confident that my taking time away from my privileged life would teach them about Jesus' love, yet they exuded His love through their evident joy, unlike anything I had ever seen before! The joy they clearly had in their hearts was what I can only describe as "shout it from the mountaintop" joy: they truly exemplified what it means to have "overflowing joy"—despite their extreme poverty.

The amount of worship and praise from the Jamaicans' joyful hearts was life-changing for me. The verse above from Philippians describes Paul in prison preaching to have joy, regardless of the circumstances. The Jamaicans I met did just that—they had joy no matter what was happening in their lives. They have inspired me to do the same, and maybe the "choose joy" mentality will just catch on everywhere!

Families

One of my favorite phrases is "Live Happy." When my kids were little, I would share pictures of them with my friends on social media tagged with #LiveHappy. After a few years of developing this mantra, I came across a cute kitchen towel that had "Live Happy" embroidered across it in bright, pretty colors. Of course, I had to buy it, and it's hanging on my towel hook in my kitchen as I type this.

Sometimes it's not so easy to "Live Happy" because things can go wrong in our lives. That's kind of where another of my favorite phrases, "Choose Joy," comes in. It's easy to be happy when things are going right! We don't usually feel happy when things don't go our way. But the Bible verses above remind us to choose to be joyful when things get tough.

That can be very hard, even for grownups! It's not easy to find joy in tough times. This reminds me of a true story I read called "The Hiding Place" by Corrie ten Boom. It is a really important book to read when you get to be an adult (if the adult reading this with you hasn't read it yet, encourage them to go check it out of the library pronto!). I want to share with you one of the parts that I shared with my own children when I read it:

Corrie ten Boom and her sister, Betsie, were imprisoned for helping people during World War II. Betsie encouraged Corrie to pray and thank God for all He had given them, even while they were in a flea-infested prison. So Corrie thanked God for everything she could think of. Betsie added that they must thank God for the fleas! Corrie went along with it but couldn't imagine why the fleas might be something to be thankful for.

Fast forward some time in the same imprisonment area. Corrie and Betsie were sharing the good news of Jesus with many, many women in the barracks with them. During this time, they would have gotten in serious trouble for sharing Jesus' love with others, but they knew it was what God had in mind for them to do. One day, a guard started to enter the prisoners' room but then refused. Why wouldn't the guard go into the barracks? Because it was swarming with fleas! The guards refused to enter their room, and therefore, the ten Boom sisters were able to minister to the other women without punishment. How many people's lives were given to Jesus due to their ministry? Thankfully, Betsie (and a reluctant Corrie) chose to find joy and thankfulness in tough times—even for the fleas!—and God protected them and used them for His purpose through it all.

Prayer

Lord God, Thank you for helping us choose to be joyful in our lives, even when things may go wrong. We thank you for being with us during good times and bad, and ask that you will help us to seek you out when we are going through those challenges. Help us to be thankful and joyful in all circumstances. In Jesus' name we pray, Amen.

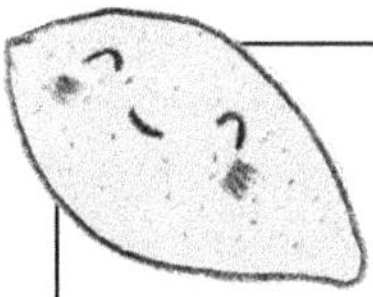

Extension Activity

Some people in our lives may need a little joy, and guess what? That is our task for today! Make a list of people you know—maybe they are neighbors, church members, teachers, friends—think outside the box! Then think of ways you might be able to bring them joy. The elderly neighbor who doesn't get out too often? Stop in with a cup of coffee and a book you could read together. The family that has six activities every night? Make them dinner and drop it off when you know they have to eat fast before practice. The friend you know who moved away? Write them an old-fashioned letter and send it to them by snail mail. Be creative about how you can share joy, and tailor it to each person's personality or needs. Who knows, maybe you'll be bringing joy to yourself while you share joy with others!

Joy

What wonders of the earth
will we see today?

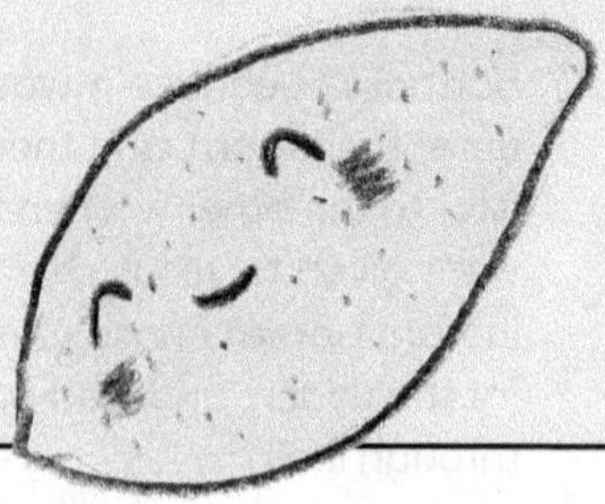

Scripture

"The whole earth is filled with awe at your wonders; where morning dawns, where evening fades, you call forth songs of joy."

– PSALM 65:8

"You make known to me the path of life; you will fill me with joy in your presence, with eternal pleasures at your right hand."

– PSALM 16:11

Parents

I am convinced that the purest form of joy on the earth can be seen through kids and dogs (well, at least our Copper ●)! Copper is now six years old but still has the energy of a one-year-old pup. As we're walking down the street, I often get asked, "Who's walking who?" as our full-of-life fifty-pound Goldendoodle leaps through the air, spins in circles, and exuberantly greets every person, car, squirrel, and blade of grass in sight, and in turn, drags me behind him. He thinks everything around him is amazing and gets overcome with joy to the extent that he loses control!

Part of the reason I have found Jack and Emmy so captivating since they were newborns is how clearly I see God's joy in them. Their first smiles came from such a pure place. The littlest things amaze them: ceiling fans, light fixtures, the sound cars make when they're honking, and seeing Christmas lights for the first time. They find wonder in what is around them and, therefore, radiate joy.

I was recently moved from my current teaching position into teaching a kindergarten classroom, and yet again, I was amazed at how naturally joy and excitement flowed through my students. They were excited about learning and had the freshest eyes. Every week we celebrated "Wonder Wednesday," where we answered one of their questions about what they were wondering... anything from how Santa gets his letters to how trampolines are made. Their curiosity and wonder about the world around them made school fun and were contagious.

This past year was such a gift in reminding me how joy and wonder go hand in hand and how God designed us to live in awe of His creation. In turn, I feel like I have learned so much from living in a state of wonder. Naturally, as we get older, more stressors exist that we didn't have to worry about as kids: being responsible for humans other than ourselves, paying bills, keeping up with endless tasks at work and in the home, etc. It is easy to become so weighed down by the duties and responsibilities of everyday life that we miss the magic unfolding right in front of us. Even my phone causes me to lose sight of wonder, missing moments with my children, the beauty of light reflecting off the lake near my house on my walking route, and other gifts God has placed in my path. I have found that the less in tune I am with God and living in awe of Him, the more **stress** I feel. The more present I am with God and find wonder in who He is and His creation, the more **joy** I feel.

God calls us in Scripture to become more like children (Matthew 18:3). Part of that is living in a state of awe and therefore receiving the joy God intended for us to find in Him and Him alone. How can we unplug, enter His presence, and receive His abundant joy today?

Families

Have you ever put on a blindfold? If not, grab a bandana and cover your eyes. How does it feel to not see anything? What do you notice?

Sometimes we live life "blindfolded" to what is right in front of us. We don't have one on, but we can get easily distracted! Technology is entertaining, but sometimes I find that it keeps me from noticing what is in front of me. Whether it is watching a movie or being on an iPad, we can be so fixed on entertainment that we miss the beautiful things God created for us to enjoy.

God tells us that in His presence is fullness of joy; that the Earth is filled with awe of His wonders. He designed us to marvel at Him and what He created and tells us that when we do, we will be filled with His joy. In His presence, He can replace any stress we feel with His joy and peace.

So, go outside today! Watch a sunrise or sunset, depending on whether you're a morning person or a night owl. *Realllyyyy* look at it and observe it. What colors did God paint across the sky? How do they change and develop as time passes? What sounds do you hear around you?

Can you believe that God created that? Can you believe that He created you?! That every cell in your body works together to allow you to live and breathe?

Live in awe today of who God is and the beautiful things He made. See what "wonders" are right in front of you. Thank Him for what you see, and receive His joy knowing that He is a creative, amazing God who made you too—uniquely and beautifully and wonderfully made!

Prayer

Dear God, We confess that sometimes we live distracted. We are blind to the wonder of your creation and who you are. Help us today to be present and seek your presence. Replace our stress with your joy, as we marvel at how wonderful and incredible you are. In Jesus' name, Amen.

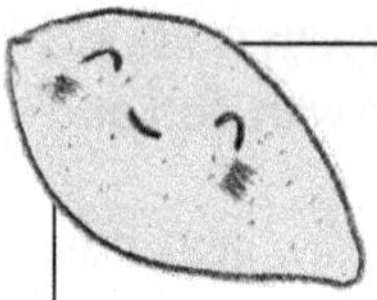

Extension Activity

Your challenge today is to unplug (and keep your parents accountable, too!). Put all phones and devices away, turn off the TV and iPads, and spend time together. *(If possible, unplug for twenty-four hours so you can really experience it! I have only done it a couple of times, but it has really blessed me and been a great technology detox!)*

Either go outside for a hike, or move your body and do a fun activity together. While outside, look around at what is in front of you. Pick a flower or cloud or plant or creature and really study it. What do you notice? How did God make it? What details did He add?

Not only can we find wonder in His nature, but we can also find it in the people He created. Maybe it is the way your brother laughs during a game or the way your mom cares for you. Do you feel more peaceful and joyful as you live in awe? See today what wonders you notice!

Peace

We have selected a *Peach* to represent *Peace*. First of all, the spellings are very similar, which we as teachers find aesthetically pleasing. Also, the light orangish color and soft peach fuzz remind us that the peace we feel can be calming, relaxing, and gentle. Lastly, you have certainly seen a peace sign—think '70s vibes! The peace sign is rounded just like the peach we have chosen to represent this Fruit of the Spirit.

Peace

God can give us peace
in every moment.

Scripture

*"As for me, I call to God, and the Lord saves me.
Evening, morning, and noon I cry out in distress, and he hears my voice.
He rescues me unharmed from the battle waged against
me, even though many oppose me."*

– PSALM 55:16–18

Parents

Take a moment and think about the following list, and consider whether you might be able to relate to any of them:

- When my kids wake me in the middle of the night
- When I am taking orders for what seems like the twenty-eighth time in the day for meal requests
- When I am unsuccessfully reasoning with my kids—yet again—about excessive TV time
- When my kids are simultaneously leaving the unwatched TV on full blast volume, singing along to Disney songs on our Bluetooth speaker, and pounding on the piano
- When my kids are in cahoots and planning some silly trick on my husband and me.

Okay, so that last one can be funny, but sometimes it seems as though our own children are against us. And if they are not against us, they seem to allow for very little "peace" in our lives—and let's be honest, parents of young children (and even older children) don't get much peace unless we seek it out. Even then, somehow our kids track us down because they want something from us. I (like many of you, I'd imagine) can't count the number of times I've asked my kids if there is anything they need, so I can take care of them before I sit peaceably and have a cup of coffee, or read, or even, you know, use the restroom for like **two seconds**... But of course, it never fails: the second I separate myself for a moment of peace and quiet, they immediately need something from me. I mean, honestly, as I've written this, there has been... ummmm... No. Peace. At. All. So yeah. That's where it's at in this parenting business.

But in these moments of unpeacefulness (which is apparently not a word, but let's pretend it is since it **so accurately** describes parenthood 99.9% of the time), this Scripture from Psalm 55 is a reminder that God is our peace whenever we cry out to Him. He hears our voice—whether we call on Him in those rare quiet moments or if we seek Him when the chaos of our lives and the world is happening around us.

And, even though it sometimes may be a challenge, let's also remember that our kids are not against us. (Okay, I'll admit it: that reminder was mostly for myself.) Yes, they bring noise and activity and, I mean, let's call it what it is: chaos. But at the same time, our children look to us for guidance, direction, support, and yes, even the peace that we have such a challenging time creating when they are around. (I remember my son, when he was four, telling me he just needed some "private time" in his room... maybe because his big sister was belting the Moana soundtrack at the top of her lungs...) Like I said, this reminder is for me as much as it is for you, to call upon God for peace whenever we feel like there is a battle against us; He will redeem our souls in peace when we ask that of Him.

Families

I want you to think about the **loudest** place you can think of. What sounds did you hear? Did you like all the noise, or did it bother you? Did you want to stay in the noise or go to a quieter place?

Now I want you to think about the quietest place you can think of. What sounds did you hear, if any? Did you like all of the quiet? How did you feel?

Our lives can sometimes be very loud, and our lives can also be quiet; both are okay. Sometimes we have louder moments than quiet ones. No matter what, whether it's noisy or quiet, we can ask God for peace in our lives. He can help us to appreciate the quiet moments and think about Him. He can also remind us in the noisy times that He is there, even with all of the loudness.

Prayer

Lord God, thank you for the peace we have in our lives that we can only get from you. We are so thankful for the quiet moments we can have with you. We are also thankful that you are with us to offer your peace, even when our lives are battling all kinds of loudness and noise. Help us to remember to call upon you for peace whenever we feel like the chaos of this life is against us. In your holy name we pray, Amen.

Extension Activity

Together as a family, go find a quiet place. It might be in your home, outside, in a park, or anywhere you can enjoy some moments of peace together. Close your eyes and breathe in the calm and peace that comes with the quiet. Take some time in quiet prayer, alone and together. Feel the peace of God surround you.

Once the peaceful time has lasted as long as your family wants it to, it's time to get loud! Turn up an upbeat song, sing at the top of your lungs, shout and yell, go for a drive with all the windows down—whatever "loud" looks like to your family. Maybe it's a very natural thing for you, or maybe you feel a little silly; either way, it's okay! At some point during the noise, take a moment to thank God that He is there with you to give you peace, even when noise surrounds you.

After you have had both the quiet and loud moments together as a family, take a minute to share with each other how you were able to find God's peace during these times. What did you notice when you called upon God for His peace? From here on out, try to share with each other when you ask God to provide you with His peace. Take notice of whether it's in times of tranquility or when it feels like things are against you, and remember: either way, His peace is there if you ask!

Peace

Peace be with you, friend.

Scripture

"Therefore, since we have been justified through faith, we have peace with God through our Lord Jesus Christ, through whom we have gained access by faith into this grace in which we now stand. And we rejoice in the hope of the glory of God."

– ROMANS 5: 1-2

Parents

Sometimes on our faith journey, God is trying to speak to us using His Word and His followers. Has that ever happened to you: you keep hearing the same message from numerous sources? You're not trying to seek it out, but somehow, it just keeps coming up from seemingly random, unexpected places? It seems like everything in your current life comes back around to that particular word, or idea, or message?

Recently, as I have delved into the Scripture and some inspiring devotionals, I have been encouraged by a certain recurring theme: peace. This theme can be found quite a bit in the Bible—maybe you've noticed, too. But when I see something continue to show up in my life, I know there's a reason. God speaks to us through His Word, through devotions that are focused on His Word, and through people who are in tune with Him; when all of these conversations and moments keep coming back to the same topic or theme, I see it as a wake-up call to listen.

Right now, there are a lot of things in my life that are not peaceful. I love my children beyond life, but I have two of the loudest children ever—one who sings and plays at the top of her lungs from the moment she's awake until the moment she sleeps; and another who, I'll be honest, is currently going through a pretty needy phase right now. I am also trying to meet the extremely challenging demands of my teaching job—any teacher reading this knows what I mean! As a side note: thank a teacher today. It goes such a long way with us!

What has been my takeaway from this constant message of "peace" that has been showing up in my life in so many ways? Well, I'll be honest. There is very little "peace and quiet" in my life. But peace doesn't necessarily have to mean calm and quiet. In fact, some unexpected faith-filled moments can take place during our loud, noisy, chaotic lives, because God is fully present with us in those moments. Whether we are in a quiet moment with Him or in the excitement happening around us, we can welcome God's peace and presence. And when we allow God's peace to infiltrate all of our attitudes and moments, we can "rejoice in the hope of the glory of God."

Families

Have you ever heard the same word or message repeated over and over again? Maybe it's the word "no" (I know parents are famous for saying this to their kids). Or maybe it's "later" or "just a minute" (again, words my kids hear from me all the time).

But sometimes the word or message that we hear repeatedly is something that God wants to share with us. (Be sure to keep in mind that it's important that we are grounded in God's Word and follow His messages, not the messages of the world. We can do this when we read the Bible and spend time with God. He can help us know how to follow Him and not just our own emotions. If you have any questions about how to do this, you can ask the wise grownups in your life to help you.) Often, when I go through something in my life, God helps me through it by sharing a repeated word, phrase, or message with me. We might hear it from our Bible, devotionals, church leaders, or families. It tends to keep showing up wherever we go, even though we're not looking for it.

Right now, I keep hearing and reading about "peace" in my Bible, devotions, and church sermons. I haven't been seeking out the topic of peace, but God knows I need to be reminded right now of the peace only He can give me.

When you hear something repeat, listen closely: Is God trying to teach you or tell you something? God puts people and situations in our lives, and uses people who follow His Word to speak to us. Use the messages He shares with you to guide you in your life.

Prayer

Heavenly Father, Help us to be in tune with the things you want us to hear. Show us your guidance through your Word and through those in our lives who follow you. Thank you for the reminder that your peace can come to us, even in the chaos of this life. In your holy name we pray, Amen.

Extension Activity

Our family loves the movie *Yes Day.* In this movie, the mother tends to tell her children "no" to everything they ask. The movie follows the family as they have "Yes Day," when the kids can decide what to do.

Maybe you've seen the movie, or maybe you have yet to watch it. Either way, decide on a "Yes Day" that your family can have together. (You may find it helpful to set parameters, like travel distance and money limits.) Then go all out and have your own Yes Day! Each time you say "yes!" to an activity, think of how God speaks to us through a repeated message or word.

Peace

May the Holy Spirit bring you
life and peace.

Scripture

"The mind governed by the flesh is death, but the mind governed by the Spirit is life and peace."

– ROMANS 8:6

Parents

One of my struggles has always been my impulse control. That cute new dress that I don't really need? Sure, why not? That impulse buy in my online cart? Yes, please. Dessert? Always. Saying no to my impulsive desires is something that I still have to work on. I've come a long way, but I'm still a work in progress. (Thank goodness for God's grace and guidance, right?)

I've noticed, though, that when I choose to spend time with God, I am more focused on His direction and less on the things I want. When my mind is focused on God and governed by the Spirit, I am offered the life and peace this verse talks about. This peace is a stark contrast to how I feel when I allow my selfish impulsivity to "govern my flesh," so to speak.

How true is it, though, that we are offered peace when we allow God to step in during moments of human weakness? I have a dear friend who gave up shopping for Lent. Inspired, I tried my own version of it. What I found (and I think my friend would agree) is that denying the superficial, instant gratification of impulse shopping gave me space to reflect on what I truly needed. It also brought a sense of peace in how I approached making a purchase of something I actually needed. I've noticed similar patterns in other areas of my life when I allow the Holy Spirit to guide my decisions, whether related to eating, shopping, or navigating healthy versus toxic relationships.

As I mentioned earlier, I believe it will be a lifelong process for me to allow my mind to be governed by the Spirit as opposed to the desires of my flesh. However, I know I gain life and peace through seeking God's guidance through his Holy Spirit.

Families

Sometimes—more often than not, really—the different Fruit of the Spirit qualities relate to each other. The verse above reminds me how peace can easily be connected to self-control. I want you to imagine the following scenarios:

You are told to wait until dinner before you have anything to eat. You know you shouldn't eat that yummy bag of your favorite snacks, but you are pretty hungry. Maybe it wouldn't hurt to just not follow your family's rules and have it real quick, before it's time to sit down at the table with your family to eat the meal that's been cooked for you. ***Crunch!*** goes your first bite of that tempting snack you've been told not to eat right now....

Same scenario, different choice: You are told to wait until dinner before you have anything to eat. Your tasty treat is calling your name, but you listen to your parents and keep the snack in the cupboard. You know you'll get to enjoy it at a later time, and it's important to listen to your parents, have self-control, and fuel your body with strong-kid food, like the meal your family cooked! You find something to do in the time that it takes to get dinner ready to eat, knowing your growling tummy and your conscience will both be happy when you sit down to dinner with your family.

In the first story, it's clear "you" made the wrong choice. Take a minute to imagine how you would feel. At first, you might be happy that you got to enjoy your snack. But before long, the guilt would set in. You'd have that sinking feeling in your stomach that you did something wrong because you *did* do something wrong. You gave in to temptation and disobeyed your parents. Your parents and God will forgive you, but I'm sure we can agree: this was the wrong move this time, wasn't it?

How about that second example, though? Great job making the right choice, hypothetical you! Sure, you didn't get your instant gratification of that special snack, even though you definitely felt hungry for it. But you showed self-control and obedience towards your parents, who are trying to help you make the decision to be healthy and strong. Even though you *wanted* that snack, you *waited* and did what you were supposed to... and it feels good! You have a sense of peace about your decision, as you very well should!

Sometimes using self-control to make the right choice can be a very hard challenge. And yes, we've all been in that first kind of imaginary scenario before, when we do something that we know we shouldn't do. But those are the times when our conscience starts an internal protest, and we feel unsettled, worried, or guilty. It's not the best feeling, knowing we should have chosen better.

But when we make the choice we know we should, our conscience remains clear. We can allow ourselves to have God's gift to us is His peace that comes with making the right decision. It's rewarding to know that, even in the times we may not *want* to make the right choice, we can be at peace about it knowing we did what's right.

Prayer

Lord God, I am so thankful for the opportunity to make the right choices in this life I'm living. I know there are times when I may struggle to make the right choice. Be with me in those moments to know that you will give me a clear conscience and peace of mind when I do what's right. Please forgive me for the times I may choose to do something that I shouldn't. Be with me and guide me to make the choices you want me to make. Thank you for your peace that comes with my self-control. In your holy name I pray, Amen.

Extension Activity

It's time for a challenge! Create a countdown anywhere from 10 to 100 (you can type in "countdown chart" online and see some images you could draw or print). Your challenge is to fill in your chart over the next week, or month, or however long it takes you to complete all those spaces. Each space can be filled in any time you recognize God's peace through choosing to have self-control. In those moments when you're tempted to choose something you shouldn't, work through it. If you'd rather turn on the TV than do your challenge, say a prayer to ask for motivation to do your task first. If you make the right choice (and I believe in you; you can do it!) then you get to fill in a space on your countdown chart.

Even if you don't always show self-control through this challenge (and you won't every time; we are not perfect, and we will make mistakes!), God offers us His forgiveness when we ask, and we have a chance to try again and make a different choice the next time. If your family is doing it together, help keep each other accountable. Ask about the wins, and work through the tough losses. In the end, it is my hope that your self-control and peace (Fruit of the Spirit) are working hand in hand to help you make the choices you should.

Peace

Where will you find peace today?

Scripture

"May the God of peace be with you all. Amen."

– ROMANS 15:33

Parents

Some years, my parents, siblings, their spouses, and all of our children go on a vacation to a destination, usually the beach. As we've grown in number, though, sometimes we do a close-to-home staycation. One day, during one of our staycations, my husband, Andy, and I went to a local restaurant to get food for the family. On our trip back, we had to travel through the valley and up a huge hill to get back to the house. As we made our way up this long, steep hill, we got stuck behind three of the slowest-moving garbage trucks I've ever encountered in my life. We were beyond frustrated, with no way around them. (I mean, we've all been in a driving situation that has frustrated us, right? No? Just me?)

By the time we returned to the rest of the family at the house, we were super annoyed. What should have taken fifteen minutes took about twice that long, maybe even longer. It was so stressful, and our moods were cranky, to say the least.

When we walked into the house, though, we encountered an even higher stress situation: my mom was visibly upset by something, and we quickly found out that she had accidentally given her password information to someone she now believed was a scammer. So she was trying to do damage control before things escalated. The family was trying to help her, but with all the kids and the excitement, it was a very chaotic scene, to say the least.

This whole turn of events reminds me that, even when things stress us out, it's important to remember that the God of peace is with us. There can always be something worse to disrupt our peace. (And honestly, it could have been way worse than even a stolen password.) God's peace is here for us, no matter what we're going through.

In the end, our family got to enjoy a delicious meal together (maybe slightly colder than we'd have hoped, but no big deal); the stolen password was able to be quickly addressed before any damage was done; and I'm guessing a lot of people's garbage was taken to the dump that day. It doesn't really change the circumstances, whether we take those opportunities to stress out or allow God's peace to carry us through them. Allow the peace of God to take you through any upsetting moments you may encounter—today and always.

Families

In my third-grade classroom, I encourage my students to work hard, make mistakes so they can learn from them, and be responsible for doing their best learning. Sometimes, I will get a student who is visibly upset or stressed. When this happens, I take a minute to talk with them and help them work through it. I teach in a public school, so I can't talk about God with my students. But I can talk about God with you here, right now. And what I want to say to you when you might find yourself in a stressful situation is that sometimes you can't change what is happening to you. Some school topics are tough. Sometimes taking tests can be stressful. Sometimes people can be mean. Sometimes bad things happen that we can't control.

What you can change, though, is how you respond to those upsetting moments. You can always ask for help: my students know they can come to me with any concerns or issues. You can also find an adult in your school or family who wants to help you. But more importantly, we can ask God to be with us in the moments we're feeling stressed or upset. The verse today is quick and to the point: it is a blessing that Paul, the Apostle, wrote in Romans to remind us that the God of peace is with us all. (Since it's so short, it might be a really easy one to memorize—want to give it a try?) When you remember that the God of peace is with you, He will help you find peace in otherwise upsetting situations. And that is a pretty amazing feeling!

Prayer

Heavenly Father, we are so thankful for the peace that you give us. Help us to remember to turn to you any time we feel upset, stressed, or angry. We know that you are the God of peace, and that you will give us your peace when we call on you. In your name we pray, Amen.

Extension Activity

Well, what do you know, it's time for a board game! In our family, we have a lot of fun playing board games together. Sometimes, though, we might get upset if we are losing or if things aren't going our way. While you play a board game together, I challenge you to ask for God's peace during those moments when you start to get upset, when things might go wrong for you. (Feel free to play as many board games as it takes before everyone playing sees both the ups and downs of it.) Moving forward, if you can think about God and His peace during a fun thing like a board game, continue to ask Him for His peace during the not-so-fun moments in life. He is with you always, and He offers you His peace.

Peace

Allow yourself to be a peace-loving peacemaker to those around you.

Scripture

"But the wisdom that comes from heaven is first of all pure; then peace-loving, considerate, submissive, full of mercy and good fruit, impartial, and sincere. Peacemakers who sow in peace raise a harvest of righteousness."

– JAMES 3:17-18

Parents

Have you ever read anything about birth order? There is some interesting research out there that suggests certain characteristics and personality traits occur, depending on what order you and your siblings were born.

I am a middle child in my sibling order, with one older sister and two younger siblings. Growing up as a middle child, I often felt like I was the last person to find anything out. I'm sure it was unintentional (or honestly, maybe my own fault for not... ahem... paying attention... or something like that.) Regardless, I remember often feeling overlooked and left out. These feelings can be typical "symptoms" of what is known as "middle child syndrome"—not an official syndrome, but some interesting theories to ponder, my fellow middle children!

No need to worry if you are also a middle child: many positive things are often attributed to middle children. Particularly, middle children have the tendency to want to mediate conflicts to help everyone come up with a mutual solution. In other words, we are peacemakers! It makes a lot of sense to me—a middle child would be "stuck" in the middle of what our younger and older siblings might want to do, so they become good at finding middle ground. Even though I may have unknowingly been the peacemaker with my siblings growing up, helping people compromise is something I continue to do to this day. As a mother and an elementary teacher, peacemaking is a very helpful skill set. Trust me—I've had to put out quite a few fires in each of those roles!

In today's culture, we often put our defenses up when conflict arises. We might feed into complaining about our boss or arguing about whether our child should be the starter on the baseball team. But what if, instead of leaning into conflict, we become the peacemakers? The Scripture above describes peacemakers in a very positive light. (Did you see that, other middle children reading this? Go us!) Like the name suggests, *peacemakers* cultivate peace (obvious, right?), and therefore—and this is big—we can yield heavenly wisdom and "a harvest of righteousness." What a positive and encouraging way to handle the conflict in our lives!

Families

Did you ever get caught in the middle of an argument? I teach third grade, and I had to help a few of my students with a problem not too long ago. Two girls were friends and usually got along really well. But I could tell that they were both upset, and a third student was trying to help them work it out.

One student (let's call her "Mary") said another student ("Anna") was being mean to her. The third girl ("Lydia") was the supportive friend who wanted to help Mary and Anna resolve their conflict, but she needed my help.

I talked to each girl privately. It turns out, Lydia and Anna were playing a game at recess, and Mary wanted to play with them, but not that particular game. In our private discussions, Mary told me that she was sad that Anna was leaving her out. Anna told me that she and Lydia wanted Mary to play with them, but they wanted to play their game. Lydia confided that she wanted to play a game with Anna *and* Mary, but then the other two girls couldn't agree on a game.

After debriefing with each girl, we all talked together. Mary's friends reassured her that they didn't want to leave her out and that they wanted to play with her. I asked if there was a way they could compromise. They decided to play Mary's game for ten minutes and then Anna's game for the rest of recess. The girls agreed that this solution would work, and they happily played at recess together for the rest of the time.

Being caught in the middle can be a tricky place to be. We want to do the right thing, but sometimes people can't agree, and then there is an argument or conflict. The Bible encourages us to be peacemakers in these circumstances. I was proud of Lydia for wanting to help her friends come to a compromise. Maybe you could be that friend sometime, too!

Prayer

Dear Heavenly Father, thank you for giving us guidance to be peacemakers in times of conflict. We pray that you will help us do as your Scripture teaches us: help us be peace-loving, considerate, submissive, full of mercy and good fruit, impartial, and sincere. Thank you for your Word that teaches us how to sow peace in order to raise a harvest of righteousness. When things happen that are not peace-filled, help us to be peacemakers and get our wisdom from you. In your holy name we pray, Amen.

Extension Activity

How about a fun game for this devotion? One of my favorite ways to work out problems or to make decisions when we can't agree is Rock-Paper-Scissors. For our Extension Activity, let's do a Rock-Paper-Scissors battle! My family likes to make a bracket and see who the ultimate winner is. (We also often recruit our stuffed animals to "play" with us, if you need a bigger group of competitors.)

For an extra bit of fun, you might want to come up with your own version of Rock-Paper-Scissors. Like, Spoon-Plate-Napkin: the spoon breaks the plate, the plate covers the napkin, the napkin wraps the spoon. Make up the motions that would go with each choice. It's okay if it doesn't totally make sense—that's part of the fun! And remember, if you ever need a fun way to be a peacemaker and help friends agree on something, Rock-Paper-Scissors is usually a pretty fair option!

Peace

Let God fill you with His peace during moments of stress and anxiety.

Scripture

"For he himself is our peace..."

– EPHESIANS 2:14

"Rejoice in the Lord always. I will say it again: Rejoice! Let your gentleness be evident to all. The Lord is near. Do not be anxious about anything, but in every situation, by prayer and petition, with thanksgiving, present your requests to God. And the peace of God, which transcends all understanding, will guard your hearts and your minds in Christ Jesus."

– PHILIPPIANS 4:4–7

Parents

I am currently sitting at the beach at Ocean City, NJ, letting the crashing sounds of the waves be my background noise as I write this devotional. Ocean City is one of my favorite places on Earth. I have been coming here with my family since I was a little girl. My dad's parents brought him here when he was a kid, he started taking us, and now I'm bringing my son here! When I was in college, I did the Ocean City Beach Project through the CCO (a Christian organization) and lived and worked here through the summer as I learned more about God, myself, and living with others in community. These sandy beaches, salty air, and boardwalk adventures ground me each summer and have seen me through so many changing seasons in my life. If I had to picture what peace looks like, my mind goes to sitting exactly here, my Bible on top of my sandy beach towel, looking out to the ocean, hearing nothing but the surf.

Ironically, on my way down to the beach, as I was trying to find the perfect place to sit and have "quiet time," I found that it was much more difficult than usual! I finally settled in and began to take a video to capture it when, all of a sudden, a loud beeping sound came from the truck clearing the beach on the sand. Moving down a bit further, I was met with T-Swift music blasting up from the boardwalk. (Don't get me wrong, I'm a big Taylor fan, but really?! at 5:30 a.m. when I'm trying to settle into my, maybe, only peaceful pocket of the day?!)

However, I'm beginning to find that this is what the pursuit of peace often looks like: appreciating pockets of it in the here and now, not in the absence of noise but in the midst of it all.

Prior to having my son, Jack, I had such a rigid routine of quiet time each morning. Before work, or in the sacred days of summer, I would start each morning slowly sipping on my coffee, filling out my gratitude journal, reading my devotional, and soaking in time in God's Word. It became a vital and essential part of my day, each day that I looked forward to and counted on. I knew that no matter how my classroom was or what happened that day, I was guaranteed twenty to thirty minutes of stillness and peace.

However, since Jack was born, this is the first full devotional I've written (he's nineteen months old!). Often, if my sweet boy isn't running around the house or babbling his first words in a language all his own, I'm either trying to catch up on sleep from a restless night, getting things ready for both of us for the day, or simply in survival mode. And if I do manage to sit down and read, it's almost guaranteed that as soon as I settle in, I'll hear a little voice or a whimper coming down the hall. It's been hard for me to find a rhythm of peace outside of my structured quiet time, with another little person in tow.

However, these past nineteen months have also taught me that maybe this is what Scripture tells us peace is: that peace isn't dependent on your circumstances. It's not found solely in quiet moments, quiet times, or simple seasons. It's not found only in stillness, in a tranquil spa, in a meditation session, or in noiseless rooms. Peace is found when we pause and breathe when we're stressed out. Peace is found when we hug our children and soak in the smell of their sweet strawberry-stained cheeks in the summertime. Peace is found when we go on a walk and submerge ourselves in nature, feeling the grass on our feet or the sand in our toes. Peace is found when we listen to worship music while driving to the grocery store. Peace is found when we feel God take over during a teachable moment in a fun and chaotic kindergarten classroom. Peace is found when we seek and experience Him. Not a perfect day, not a perfect moment, but He Himself is a perfect God who is always present and always here and gave up His life for us so that we could live in His love, with the absence of fear, and experience His peace eternally.

So today, wherever you are and regardless of your schedule and circumstances, pause for a second, quiet your mind, take a breath, and picture Jesus sitting next to you. Whether you picture Him with you on the beach at Ocean City or by your side on a mountaintop, know that as you pursue Him, you will find peace, for He Himself is your peace.

Families

Have you ever been so worried about something that it's hard to fall asleep? Maybe it's a thunderstorm that is so loud outside, a big test in school, or you feel lonely and afraid? I know I have! For me, I have always been so afraid to let others down that I can get nervous and lose sleep over worrying about that happening! It is hard to fall asleep, let alone feel peaceful, when you are scared, anxious, or afraid!

Did you know, though, that the Bible tells us that we don't need to be anxious about anything? Remember Paul, whom we talked about earlier—the man who was imprisoned but said no matter our circumstances, we could find joy? He said a few verses earlier that through praying to God, thanking Him for who He is, and sharing every fear of ours (big and little!), He will take out our fears in our minds and hearts and replace them with His peace. Knowing that He is always with us, that He loves us, and that He is working all things together for something good allows us to have one of His greatest gifts: His peace.

So, the next time you feel a little scared, or worried, or anxious, stop and talk to God! Even if it seems small, nothing is too small or too big for God—He cares about it all, and He cares about you! He is your peace.

Prayer

Dear God, thank you for the gift of your peace. Thank you for the reassurance that when we share what we're scared about with you, you will listen and replace our fears with your comfort and peace, letting us know that we're never alone. Thank you that you are our peace. Help us to seek you in our busy moments today. In Jesus' name, Amen.

Extension Activity

Find a favorite spot, whether it's in your house, at a park, or in your yard! Bring some paper, crayons, or a marker and yourself! Set your timer for five minutes and just be with God! Draw or write about something you're nervous about, close your eyes, and listen to the sounds of the birds outside, feel God's creation surrounding you. Color a picture or just sit and rest. Once the five minutes are up, notice how you feel! Do you feel more peaceful and calm?

Patience

For *Patience,* we chose to use a *Watermelon.* We like to think that, as we patiently pick out watermelon seeds before taking a bite of the juicy fruit, we can be reminded that having patience in our lives can often yield sweet results.

Patience

God will give you the strength and patience you need.

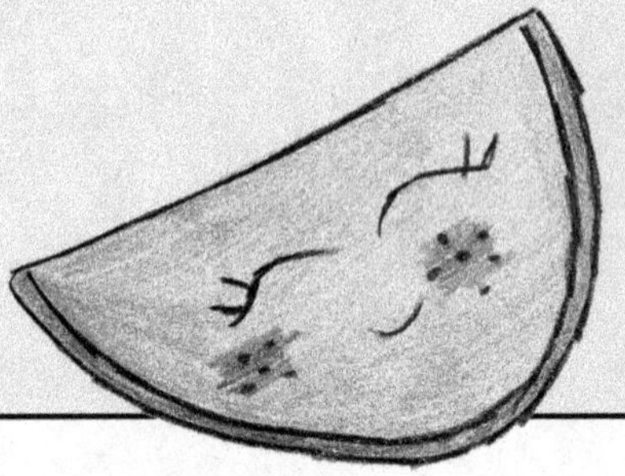

Scripture

"But those who hope in the Lord will renew their strength.
They will soar on wings like eagles;
they will run and not grow weary,
they will walk and not be faint."

– ISAIAH 40:31

Parents

One day, I was feeling very impatient. It didn't matter if things were going right or wrong for me; I had woken up with a very impatient attitude. There was quite a bit of stress I was dealing with for that particular chapter of life: I had a lot going on with work due to COVID, and our family was all quarantining and social distancing. The kids were doing virtual learning, my husband was working remotely, and I was teaching my own virtual instruction for my third-grade classroom. The global crisis impacted every family we knew in many devastating ways... Fortunately, we were healthy and safe, but trying to work things out with our new temporary (we hoped!) normal. It was unlike anything I'd ever had to do for my job before, and there was not enough time to get it done the way I'd normally expect from myself. To top it off, I had two loud and excited kids who needed me (or "needed" me) every time I thought I had a free second. I was out of patience and trying not to completely fall apart. It wasn't going well.

"Mom?" uttered my five-year-old for what seemed like the millionth time.

"What!?!" I *almost* shouted back at him. I wasn't in the mood for anything. At all. It was one of those moments.

I actually, very gently, replied, "What do you need, honey?"

Thank goodness I had changed my tune in time, because he sweetly said to me, "I love you more than the stars and the world and the **universe**!"

If you can't already tell from some of the stories I've shared, my youngest child is full of sweet things to say about his momma. (Let me be clear: He also has plenty of not-so-sweet moments where he tests my patience.) Fortunately, I didn't let on that my patience was wearing thin when I answered him. With his loving words as a reminder that the Lord will give us what we need to renew our strength, any patience I had been losing just moments earlier was replenished.

Having patience on even our best days is sometimes a challenge. On those not-so-great days, patience can be the last thing on our minds. But isn't the message that this Scripture above shares so freeing? At the same time, isn't it also so challenging to keep our "hope in the Lord" to renew our strength, especially at those moments when we feel like we're at the end of our rope? The metaphor of soaring on wings like eagles: what a beautiful, freeing concept! And then taking it a step further to say that our hope in the Lord allows us to run and not grow weary, to walk and not be faint... yes, that's how I feel when I am truly hoping in the Lord! When I remember that my hope is in Him, I don't lose perspective and patience. But what a challenge that can be in the moments when my hope and patience wear thin.

I'm not sure what caused me to pause and have patience with my son when he said my name in the story I shared above. I know there have been plenty of other times when I've snapped at him impatiently when he asked for something, and I'm not proud of those reactions.

Sometimes, the burden of our lives becomes overwhelming, at the very least. We lose patience with those we love, and we let the weight of it all start to take over. I do know that the Lord gives us freedom from our impatient moments when we hope in Him. I pray that when you find yourself in those moments of feeling worn down, impatient, and overwhelmed, you find hope in the Lord, like this verse says. In those moments, may we all put our hope in Him and feel as free as if we were soaring on wings like eagles.

Families

What do you think it would be like to "soar on wings like eagles"? Would it be fun? My five-year-old, as I mentioned in the Parents Devotional, says, "I would feel free!"

I definitely agree! It would be an adventure, and we would be "free as a bird!" (which is a fun expression some people say that absolutely applies here!).

Sometimes it's hard to feel free. There might be things bothering us and causing us to become impatient. We might have a bad day. We might be upset by something a friend or family member said or did. We might just feel tired and annoyed for no particular reason.

God wants us to know that when we put our hope in Him, He will "renew our strength" and help us not be weary or tired. So the next time you are feeling down, impatient, or sad, try to remember the Bible verse above. Know that God will help you feel as free as if you were soaring like an eagle! He will give you the strength and patience you need.

Prayer

Heavenly Father, we are so grateful that you offer freedom to us when we place our hope in you. Please help us to remember that when we feel overwhelmed, worn down, and impatient with the things around us, when we are growing weary from our lives, we can hope in you. Help us ask you for the strength we need so we can feel as free as eagles soaring. In your holy name, Amen.

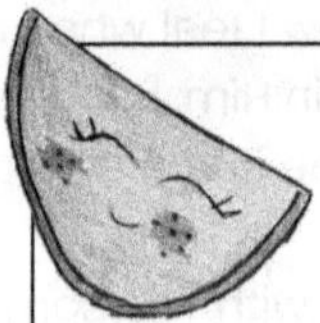

Extension Activity

The Scripture above talks about eagles, and we took some time imagining we were soaring on wings like eagles today. There is actually a huge eagle's nest not far from our house, and sometimes we're lucky enough to see those beautiful birds soaring freely through the sky! So for our activity today, it's time for a nature walk! Go outside—maybe a park, a hiking trail, the woods, or just around where you live—and look for any plants and animals you can find in nature. God has given us so many beautiful plants and animals in His creation. You can choose how you want to appreciate nature on your nature walk. Maybe you'll take a journal and write down a list of the plants and animals you see or how they make you feel. Perhaps you'll draw pictures of the things you find. You might choose to bring a camera to photograph the beauty of creation. Or maybe you'll just take your nature walk as a special time to be together with your family. You are sure to see things you probably never noticed before! Who knows, maybe on your nature walk, you'll see some eagles, too!

Patience

Long-suffering is the kind of patience
we can ask for from God
when we go through hard times.

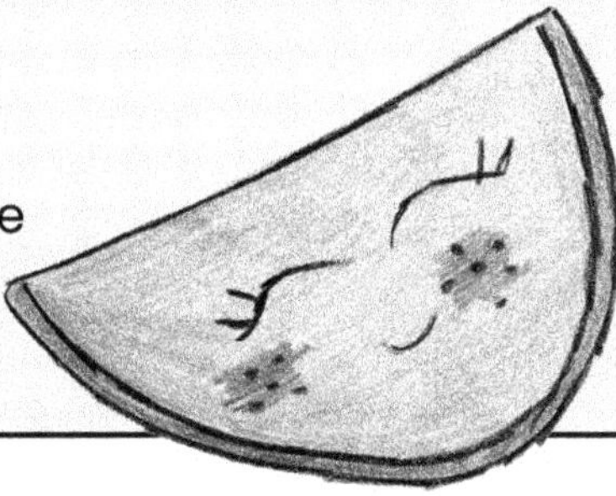

Scripture

"Praise be to the God and Father of our Lord Jesus Christ, the Father of compassion and the God of all comfort, who comforts us in all our troubles, so that we can comfort those in any trouble with the comfort we ourselves receive from God. For just as we share abundantly in the sufferings of Christ, so also our comfort abounds through Christ. If we are distressed, it is for your comfort and salvation; if we are comforted, it is for your comfort, which produces in you patient endurance of the same sufferings we suffer. And our hope for you is firm, because we know that just as you share in our sufferings, so also you share in our comfort."

– 2 CORINTHIANS 1:3-7

Parents

I don't know about you, but one of the most challenging questions I hear as a Christian is, "Why do bad things happen to good people?" Often, this question is asked by someone who is coming from a place of hurting or loss. This pain might be something they personally are going through or something they might be watching a loved one endure.

From an outsider's perspective, it might seem like people who are in touch with Jesus should be exempt from the bad things that could happen to them. This, as you may know, is not the case.

As someone who has dealt with my fair share of bad things, I know from firsthand experience that bad things can happen to anyone. At the same time, I know that the "bad" things I've experienced may pale in comparison to others' who are much "better" than I am. In fact, looking at some of the "best" people in the Bible, many of them had bad things happen to them beyond what I can even fathom... not to mention that the only perfect human who ever existed—Jesus—suffered and died the most horrific death imaginable!

In the King James Version of the Bible, the word "long-suffering" can be found in place of the word "patience" in the Fruit of the Spirit passage. The interpretation I have of the word "long-suffering" is a bit literal: suffering for a long time, particularly when challenging things happen that we may have to be patient with. Whether it's the suffering or pain of a loved one, the loss of a child, marriage struggles, job challenges, or whatever trial or difficulty we can fill in the blank with, long-suffering is enduring something painful. So why is long-suffering listed as one of the traits we should try to have, right alongside the other positive Fruit of the Spirit characteristics, like joy and love?

Long-suffering and its sister word, patience, go hand in hand. No one will go through this life without difficulties. At some point, we will all be faced with something "bad"—no matter how "good" we might be. (Yes, I'm keeping in mind that we are all sinners and far from perfect; thus, the quotation marks.) Long-suffering is the kind of patience that we can only get from God. It allows us to have the godly kind of patience we need to have and share with others, especially in difficult times.

The Scripture above describes patient endurance in times of suffering. It reminds us that God is with us as we suffer and that He is also with us to share in times of comfort from those sufferings. We can be there to share this news with others as they endure the difficulties life brings them. And when bad things happen to anyone, we are able to seek the comfort that only God can give us.

Families

Have you ever had something bad happen to you? Maybe you have lost a loved one. Maybe your friends were mean to you. Maybe you have gotten sick or have really gotten hurt. Maybe you've even broken a bone. Maybe you have had a pet that died. No matter how hard we might try, it's impossible to avoid the difficulties life brings us.

What do you do when something bad happens to you? The Scripture above tells us that we can have a special kind of patience when things go wrong. (Another word for this can be "long-suffering"—maybe you've heard that word before!)

Sometimes when I'm going through a challenging time, I find someone whom I can talk to about it. It doesn't magically make things all better, but I have found it helps to go through something hard with someone else by my side.

When something goes wrong, God is by our side to give us comfort. We can comfort others who are going through troubles too, because God gives us all comfort when we go through something bad in our life. When we have patience even in those difficult times, God will be there to give us comfort. And even though it may not make the bad thing go away, having God by our side will give us the comfort that only He can give.

Prayer

Heavenly Father, we are so grateful for the comfort that only you can give us in hard times. Help us remember to ask you to be by our side when we go through the challenges of this life. Help us to be there for others in their times of trouble, and to remind them that you can be their comfort. In your name we pray, Amen.

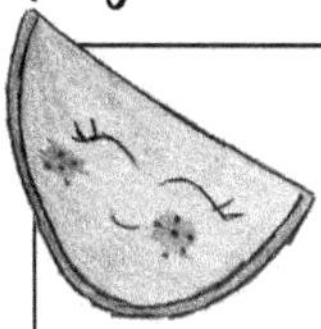

Extension Activity

Some older people in your community may live in a retirement home. Often these people may feel lonely, especially as they may have to go through difficult times in their lives.

For this Extension Activity, find a local retirement community and set up a visit with the residents who live there. Some retirement homes have volunteers and visitors who help out, so ask what your family could do for the people who live there. Maybe you'll be able to sing or play a game with them, or even just talk with them for a while. And who knows? You may make some new friends there in the meantime!

Patience

Be quick to listen and
slow to speak.

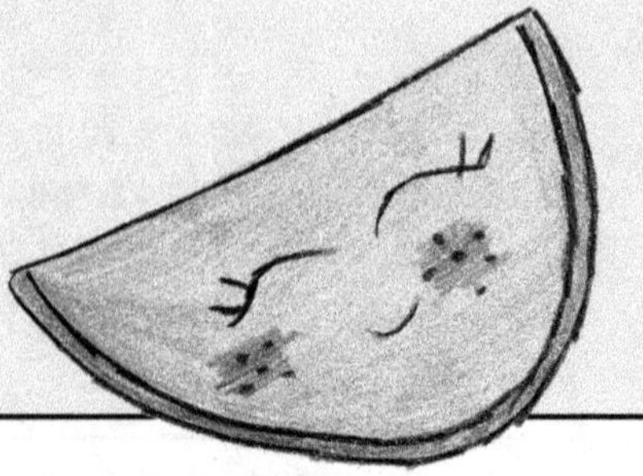

Scripture

"I waited patiently for the Lord;
He turned to me and heard my cry."

– PSALM 40:1

Parents

I have been working on my habit of interrupting others when they are talking. I am aware that I have the tendency to get excited about what someone is talking about (not a bad thing!). But then I interject my own thoughts or opinions or stories (which I know can be super rude, so that's why I'm working on it...).

Recently, I heard the quote, "God gave us two ears and one mouth," in reference to listening before speaking. As a habitual interrupter, I had a minute to step back and reflect on what kind of listener I truly am. When my husband tells me about his day, am I hearing him out when he tells me what brought him joy or frustrations? Or am I quick to insert my own anecdotes about my day? When my coworkers tell me about their exciting holiday plans, am I giving them a chance to share? Or am I quick to jump in about my own fun plans? When my children tell me about what's bothering them at school, am I listening with both ears to their experiences? Or am I using my one quick-tongued mouth to quickly try to come up with an idea to tell them how to fix their problems?

I *should* know better. When I share with someone, if they don't hear me out... or give me a chance to express my thoughts fully... or allow me space to vent, I get discouraged. We all want to be heard, and we all should be given space to share our voice. It feels reassuring to be able to speak our piece.

The Scripture above reminds us that when we wait patiently for the Lord, he hears us. What a good reminder to also be a patient listener to others around us, so we can be a Godly example to them.

Families

Have you ever been interrupted by someone? It doesn't feel good when someone cuts you off, so you can't finish what you want to say. How do you feel when someone doesn't give you a chance to tell them what you think? It can be upsetting and frustrating, and it might discourage you from wanting to speak up in the future.

A quote I heard recently made me think about how important it is to listen to others. The quote is: "God gave us two ears and one mouth." This reminds me that I should use my two ears to listen first. Then, after my friend has had a chance to express what they want to me, I can use my one mouth to talk about it with them.

God is the most patient listener of all, because He listens to us whenever we talk to Him. He is patiently waiting to hear everything we want to share with Him. He is the best example for us all when it comes to being a good listener.

Prayer

Heavenly Father, thank you for listening to us anytime we need you. Help us to remember that you are always patiently waiting to hear from us. Help us to be a patient listener too, one who is quick to listen and slow to speak. Help the words we say to others be a reflection of you in our hearts. In your name we pray, Amen.

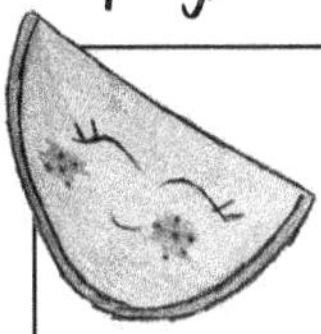

Extension Activity

Sometimes it's hard to wait to take your turn to speak when someone else is talking. This week, let's try something new during the conversations we find ourselves in: instead of talking quickly when a friend tells you something, do the "pause-nod" move instead. As someone is speaking to you, when they come to a brief pause; simply nod your head. They may continue to share more about what they wanted to tell you. When there is another pause, nod again. Try not to say anything at all and see if they keep talking. After they are truly done because they stop talking, affirm their words by saying, "Thank you for telling me that," or, "I appreciate you sharing with me." Maybe you will be an inspiration for all the people you know to be good listeners, too!

Patience

Be patient, not proud.

Scripture

"The end of something is better than its beginning.
Patience is better than pride."

– ECCLESIASTES 7:8

Parents

In my recent adult years, I have become involved in local theater. Several years ago, my daughter, with her flair for the dramatic and natural performing talents, auditioned for her first stage show. Prior to one of the performances, the director asked me to fill in for a small role for one night. I resisted at first, but then decided, *Hey, why not?* So I put on my costume and stage makeup, stepped on stage, said my five or so lines that I'd quickly memorized, and performed for a real live audience! At that moment, I realized that this might be something I want to do again. Performing for a live audience gave me energy, and being in shows fulfilled a desire I didn't know I had.

Since that first small fill-in role, I have been able to perform on stage in many different capacities: some lead roles, some very minor parts, some musicals, some straight plays, and quite a few improv performances—kind of a little bit of everything.

I've learned a lot through theater, a lot of which relates to the Scripture verse above. See if you can find some of the same connections:

- There is a significant and obvious improvement from the very first rehearsal through the actual performance. It's incredible to see the change from start to finish!
- If I have an elevated ego about my ability to play a part well, that doesn't help me improve my roles. (This realization is a necessary reflection on pride and how it doesn't have a place on the stage.)
- Likewise, when crafting my characters, I have to be patient to see how the character develops. If I'm prideful from the start that I have it "all figured out," there is a rude awakening at some point in the process when I have to pivot.
- I have to have patience and trust in the director and their vision for the bigger picture.

- I have to be careful not to get overly confident or too proud because mistakes can and will happen. For example, I had memorized one particular line months prior to the performance. But on opening night, I totally blanked on it. Thankfully, my castmates were able to cover and get me right back on. But that's humbling.
- Hard work and patience in the process yield good results.

This (somewhat lengthy) metaphor reminds me of the truth in the verse above. In a much bigger way, the end of things God leads us through in our lives is better than the beginning, because we have the promise of eternal life with him. Similarly, it is a good rule to live by patience instead of pride. Instead of being prideful and pursuing what we think we should, we should be patient with God to pursue His will for our lives.

Families

Do you like to put on shows? My daughter, Aila, has always been a performer. She has been on stage in various roles from a very young age: acting, dancing, singing. When she can't be on stage, she makes her own stage, insisting, "Mom! Watch this!" and showing off her latest flip, song, or trick.

When Aila was very little, she took dance and gymnastics classes. She also did very small roles in theater performances. She did a great job, especially for her age.

However, as she has gotten older, I have been so impressed with the skills she has learned. Her dance moves have become very strong, and her gymnastics tricks have become more impressive. Her theater roles have been more challenging, and she has risen to the occasion to perform them amazingly.

It's so interesting to look back on how far she has come! At her first gymnastics classes, I was so impressed when she did a little somersault. Now she flips and spins like it's nothing. It's a great reminder that, while we all start somewhere, the end is better than the beginning. Whatever circumstances we find ourselves in life, God is with us from beginning to end, and what a promising reminder that the end will be better than the beginning!

Prayer

Dear God, You are with us in every circumstance. Whatever we are going through, thank you for being with us, and for the reminder that however bad or good the beginning is, the end will be even better. Help us to remember to be patient and not proud, and to do the things you want us to in order to do your will and bring glory to you. In your holy name we pray, Amen.

Extension Activity

Talent show time! This Extension Activity may take a bit longer than some of the others. Each person will decide on the talent that they would like to perform. (Feel free to invite other extended family members, neighbors, or friends to join in the fun!) Set aside a little time each day to practice your performance. After about a week, perform for each other! Reflect on the gifts and talents God gave you all, and think about how much your performance has improved from beginning to end.

Patience

Be patient, even when things might not be going the way you want them to.

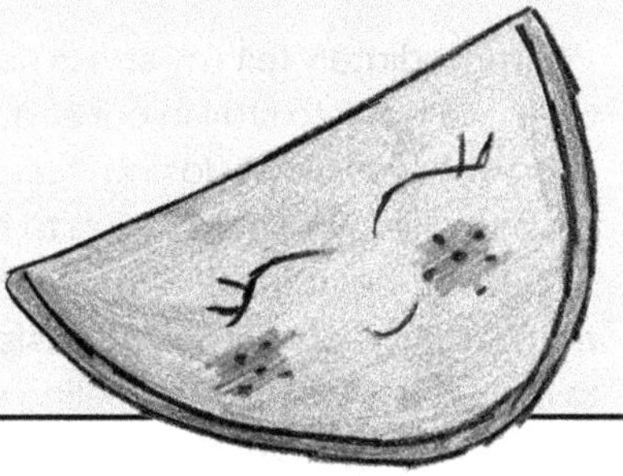

Scripture

"Fixing our eyes on Jesus, the pioneer and perfecter of our faith."

– HEBREWS 12:2

Parents

Yesterday, we flew home from a wonderful week at one of our favorite vacation spots: Disney World. It was so much fun, but also exhausting!! Vacations with kids aren't quite as relaxing as they used to be, let alone at fast-paced and *so-much-to-do-and-see* Disney World!

Coming back, we were all tired, drained, and ready to make it back. I don't know about you, but I'm always a little sad when vacation is over, and when I get to the airport, I am ready to get home as quickly as possible. However, at airports, that is seldom the case.

Our flight was scheduled for a 3:45 departure, and when we got to the airport, it was pushed back to 4:20. The delay wasn't too bad, so I tried to strategically spend our airport time in a way that would help set up our twenty-month-old for a successful flight. I fed him at exactly the right time so that his belly would be full during the flight, I took him on walks to get his energy out, we changed his diaper right before we boarded... Everything was lining up perfectly for a happy baby (and therefore less stressed us and fellow plane passengers).

We got on the plane, got our movie ready, and Josh and I were feeling pretty good! Things were looking up! We went through the safety instructions with the flight attendants, they did seat checks, the cabin lights went out, we got ready for departure, and then twenty minutes passed, which turned into thirty... Finally, the pilot came on and said we were eighteenth in line to leave the runway, so it should probably be another fifteen to twenty minutes.

At this point, I got out some snacks for Jack to distract him from throwing his binkies everywhere, opening and shutting the airplane window as hard as he could 1,000 times, and kicking the seat in front of us. Fifteen to twenty more minutes were manageable—we could do this!

But then the time passed, and it turned into another thirty. The pilot got on again and said that they had closed the runway due to weather, and we would have to wait it out. This was not what we had planned!!!

I immediately felt my stress rising—how much longer could I entertain Jack when we have to stay in our seats? Babies around the plane were crying, and everyone was slowly losing their cool. Eventually two hours passed before we were finally given permission to take off.

Despite having a few moments of total overwhelm, Jack did surprisingly well and, by God's grace, fell asleep for the last hour of the flight, allowing me to rest. At this point, after feeling exhausted, stressed, impatient, and worried, I allowed myself to take a deep breath.

Reflecting on the experience, I realized how hard it is to be patient when things go wrong. I try so hard to control the experience and make it go perfectly, but when things are suddenly out of your control, it's really hard to regroup and relax as you have to wait for His timing. I also realized through the plane adventure how my natural human instinct is to get mad at the situation and stressed. It is so hard in the heat of the moment to do what Hebrews calls us to do and "fix our eyes on Jesus."

Yesterday was such a good reminder to me that we are not in control, and we need the Lord each moment to supply us with what we need (patience, strength, etc.) When we want to tap out, it is the perfect time to tap into the ultimate supplier of limitless patience and strength. When we fix our eyes on Him, He can give us what we need, help change our perspective, and even flood us with the Fruits of the Spirit that don't come naturally during times of stress and distress.

Families

Have you ever been to an amusement park? My family and I just went to our favorite theme park—Disney World! Jack is now almost two and was so excited to ride the rides—especially the carousel, *Dumbo,* and *Winnie the Pooh!*

If you've ever been to Disney World, or a fair, or an amusement park, you know that sometimes you have to wait in line for the ride that you want to get on. It can be a quick wait, and you can get on in five minutes, but sometimes it can be a very long wait. Once, I had to wait in line for almost three hours to ride *Avatar* when it first opened!

When you have to wait, it can be really hard to be patient, especially when you're excited. I sometimes catch myself watching the people ahead of me board the ride, feeling a little jealous, wishing it were me instead. Have you ever felt that way?"

Sometimes in life, we have to wait for things that we're excited about and really want to happen. It is easy to want to wish time away or have it happen sooner. However, God has things He wants to teach us and show us where we are now, and if we aren't patient, we may miss what gifts He has for us while we wait. Rather than looking at the people ahead of you in line with jealousy, fix your eyes on Jesus. He has some wonderful things planned for you on the way to the ride!

Prayer

Dear God, sometimes it can be really hard to be patient and wait for the things we hope to happen or are excited for. Please give us patience while we wait, and eyes to see what you are trying to teach us. Sometimes the journey is just as important as the destination, and we pray that you will help us fix our eyes on you through it all. In Jesus' name, Amen.

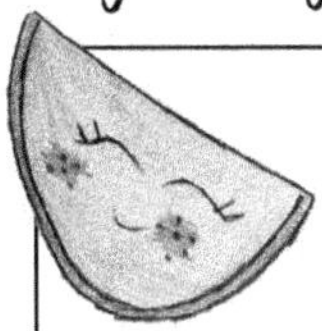

Extension Activity

This week we are going to take a field trip to the local library! Just like Jesus wants us to fix our eyes on Him, we are going to practice with some books where patience and focus are key!

Check out any of the *I Spy* books or an optical illusion book from the library. These books require you to fix your eyes on the page to find the hidden pictures *(I Spy),* or for the optical illusion books, the more you look at the pictures, the more they change and transform. For either, if you are not patient or don't focus in, you won't be able to get the full effect or find what is missing.

Have fun, and as you do it, think about what it looks like to fix your eyes on Jesus! What might He try to show you when you do?

Patience

Pursue joy, patience, and faith in your life.

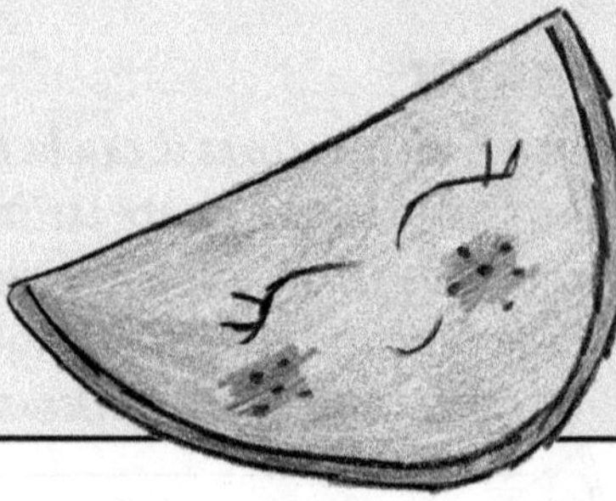

Scripture

"Be joyful in hope, patient in affliction, faithful in prayer."

– ROMANS 12:12

Parents

It is July of 2023, and we are currently on our family's staycation. It was on this staycation in the summer of 2020 that the idea for this book was born—poolside! Since then, over the past few years, we have slowly been plugging away at it. These devotions have been written through many life events: children growing up and beginning activities they're passionate about, a child being born and another on the way, continuing careers, and going on different adventures. It has seen us through highs and lows and changes, and some things that never change. It has been surreal rereading the devotionals written three years ago and reentering the place and mindset in which they were written.

There have been seasons where we've been able to write a lot and seasons where months have passed before picking up our phones, iPads, or laptops to create another devotional. Sometimes these have been written in one sitting during nap time, while other times they've been written in ten-minute segments whenever we can take a breath. It has been a long journey. (Here I am trying to finish writing this paragraph, which I started five hours ago—after getting interrupted to make breakfast, second breakfast, endless snacks, and trips inside and outside, without having had my morning coffee and running on very minimal sleep. ● Needless to say, today I am in desperate need of God's gift of patience.)

But here we are! Even though you are only partway through this book, this is our last devotional that we are writing for it. And it seems fitting that the last one we are writing has to do with patience, as it, like most big endeavors, has required a lot of patience to complete this project: patience with ourselves, patience with one another, and patience with our circumstances. I think patience often is the key to flexibility, and where I can have the tendency to be rigid and structured with my time, even through this project, God has taught me a lot in how to be flexible and patient with giving Him control of how my days and time are spent (as they often differ from my expectations).

Through God giving me patience and perseverance, I have often found that there are so many blessings I encounter in their wake. Even through writing these excerpts, God has flooded me with His peace, reminders of His goodness, love, and faithfulness, and replaced anxiety with joy, even when I was tired, drained, or felt like I didn't have much to give. I often find that when God puts something on your heart, even if it seems like a long and impossible task, He will make a way and bless you with His supernatural good fruits in the process. He plants hope and a vision in our hearts and, through prayer, is capable of giving us the patience we need to fulfill the great plans He has for us. Spend some time with the Lord today and listen for what He is calling you to do. It is my prayer that He will bless you in ways you couldn't imagine in the process of surrendering to His plan.

Families

I was driving my eight-year-old son to my parents' house, about an hour and a half away. I was stressed because my GPS had me arriving three minutes late for my grandma's 90th birthday celebration. As a child, my family of six was often late, which was very upsetting; now, as an adult, I get very anxious and overly stressed when I'm running late for anything. As I drove on the highway, I kept commenting on other drivers: how they were in my way, or couldn't pick a speed, or were driving in the right lane.

After about half of our drive, my boy called me out on it. He asked me why I was being so mean to the other drivers. I tried to justify what I was saying by explaining that I just wanted to get there safely and as quickly as possible. "But you were still being mean."

He was absolutely right, and I told him that. I said I'm sorry (I think it's extremely important to apologize to my kids when I do something wrong; that could be a whole different devotion in itself!). Then I thanked him for reminding me to be patient. Here we were, my son and I, with some rare quality one-on-one time, and instead of enjoying his "Awesome Jams Playlist" and talking about whatever came up, I was commenting impatiently about the questionable driving abilities of my fellow drivers. I fine-tuned my patience and had a nice rest of the drive with my boy.

Yes, I was channeling my patience. Look at me go!

Days later, I somehow got lumped into being the babysitter by default for a ton of kids just because I was the only adult around.

Then a friend made a well-intentioned but super-annoying request of me.

After that, I had to do things for my job that I was not at all ready for (I mean, this teacher on summer break was *not* feeling it.)

But I'm patient! Ugh!!!

Okay, so this is where I need to remember that my patience is not mine at all! Every day, things will happen and will be frustrating. There are way too many things that irritate me on a regular basis, so being fully patient is a terrible challenge for me. So that's when I need to be faithful in prayer to be patient with the things that come up and test me. God is with me in those moments when I can only find patience through His help.

Essentially, our earthly journey is similar to the road trip with my son: filled with moments that test our patience. We can pray to ask God to help us have patience in the moments that we need it along the way.

Prayer

Dear God, life can be busy and crazy sometimes. Often our days do not reflect what we have planned or what we hope to happen. They are filled with moments, situations, and projects that stretch us and challenge us. It is easy to become bitter, angry, and defeated. Please give us the patience to not only complete the tasks you have for us but also complete them with a joyful heart. Allow these patience-building opportunities to make us more like you. In Jesus' name, Amen.

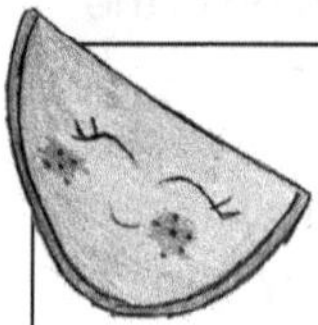

Extension Activity

For this activity, we thought it would be funny to encourage you to go on a family camping trip and see how your patience is tested. (This may seem a little extreme! ● But if you're feeling it, go for it!) Throughout your camping trip, take notice of your patience and—let's be real—its limits in key camping moments. We wonder if you'll need to channel your patience when you set up a tent. Or maybe you'll need extra patience while that pesky rock pokes you under your pillow as you try to sleep. We can imagine patience would also come in handy as you're slowly cooking food over a temperamental campfire... There are so many opportunities for your patience to shine on a camping trip! Go on, pack your Patient Pants, and let us know how it goes—you've got this!

For our non-camping fans who prefer a slightly simpler activity, try this instead. First, split your family into two teams. You will need one small ball per team and one timer (phones will work). The objective is to get as many catches in a row as possible before the five minutes run out.

- Set your timer for five minutes.
- Count how many times you and your teammates can toss the ball back and forth without dropping it.
- Keep track of your highest score, and see if you can beat it! Whichever team has the highest number of catches is the winner.

Was it hard to stay patient with your teammate(s) as you were tossing the ball back and forth? What about when you or your teammate messed up? Was it difficult being patient with your teammate and yourself, especially when there were only five minutes to try and earn points? Talk over these questions, and use them to inspire a plan that channels your patience when you most need it. (The campers who barely got any sleep at the campsite last night know what we're talking about!)

And, hey, at least you picked the simpler Extension Activity option, and we didn't force you to be a happy—and patient—camper! (For the record, we love camping. We totally recommend it. So why don't you grab your tent and give that camping thing a try now, too, if you can! And again, don't forget to pack those Patient Pants. We're guessing you'll need them.)

Kindness

Kindness is represented in this book as a *Pineapple*. Being kind sometimes means standing up (nice and tall, like a pineapple does) to express kindness towards someone. We can also look at the pineapple and remember not to be prickly, like the pineapple's exterior, but instead to be sweet and kind like the fruit inside.

Kindness

Speak kind things and be glad!

Scripture

"Anxiety in a man's heart weighs him down,
but a good word makes him glad."

– PROVERBS 12:25

Parents

A year or so ago, I had a beautiful moment with my son. I had been anxious and frustrated about whatever that day's tasks were, so I just tried to "fake it" as I went about my day. My son, however, was as content as could be in our car as we drove. He was admiring the lovely flowers our town had displayed in the center roundabout, around a quaint, small town clock tower. It's a really gorgeous display, and the flowers were especially pretty, so what Archie said next really made my heart smile: "Those flowers remind me of how much I love Mommy."

Well. Four-year-olds can just make you melt, am I right? He may not always be that sweet (though he's definitely a sweetheart most of the time), but in that moment, his kind words made my heart beyond glad. I could truly feel the anxieties and frustrations of my day float away as they were replaced with gladness in my heart.

This particular verse from Proverbs is a huge reminder that anxiety does not have a place in our hearts if we hope to be unburdened from the weight it brings to our lives. The second part of this verse, however, is where the "action" starts—a good word makes him glad! What a positive reminder that we can use a kind word in our life! And what better way to spread kindness than by saying a good word to someone else? Just like my boy did for me that memorable day, we have the potential to give someone the gift of gladness by doing the simplest thing—saying something nice to them. When we pump positivity into other people's lives, sometimes we can visibly see the weight of their anxiety lift off of that person; other times, we may not know the impact it may have on them. We don't know the journey that person may be on and the anxieties that may come with it, but what we do know is this: a good word makes them glad.

Families

Sometimes things in our lives make us feel worried or anxious. Have you ever felt that way? Was there anything that helped you feel better when you were worrying?

Take a second to think of a time when someone said something kind to you. How did it make you feel? The Bible verse today tells us that a good word makes us glad! I would guess you felt pretty glad when that person said a kind thing to you.

Now, I want you to think of a time you said something kind to someone else. How did it make you feel? How do you think it made them feel? Most likely, the same thing happened to them! They probably felt really glad that you said that kind thing to them. And you probably also felt pretty great, since you were sharing kindness with someone!

Kindness may seem like a really easy thing to do, but sometimes we may forget to offer kindness to our neighbor. So remember, this world can never have enough kindness, so be kind to others whenever you can!

Prayer

Lord God, thank you for giving us the gift of kindness. Help us to be kind to each other. Help us to remember to offer a kind word to others. Help us to have people in our lives who can offer us a kind word, especially when we are feeling anxious. Thank you for helping us show your love to others when we offer them kindness. In your holy name we pray, Amen.

Extension Activity

As a family, keep a Kindness Journal! If you have a blank journal or notebook, great, use that! Or be creative—you can make one out of several sheets of blank paper folded in half, type it on your computer, save it as a note in your phone, or use whatever you have! Each time you say or do something kind to someone else, write it down in your Kindness Journal. When someone says or does something kind to you, write it down in your Kindness Journal. Before you know it, you will be finding kind moments in ordinary, everyday life! Feel free to look back on these moments of kindness whenever you need a pick-me-up, and remember to offer kindness to those around you every chance you get!

Kindness

Be thankful! Appreciate the kindness you receive.

Scripture

"Give thanks in all circumstances; for this is God's will for you in Christ Jesus."

– 1 THESSALONIANS 5:18

Parents

I'm about to admit something that will make me sound very silly. Okay, here goes nothing: I struggle immensely with making beds and with bedding in general. Now I get to explain (and I promise, I will continue to sound like a ridiculous human... there are very few redeeming moments in the following description).

When my husband, Andy, and I were first married, I think he thought I was joking around when I made the bed. The sheets would be tangled (I promise, I tried to straighten them!). The comforter would be crooked (I may or may not have tried to stack my side to have a bit more fabric). The pillows were... well, those were okay. But it's hard to mess up pillows.

If I were the one in charge of replacing the sheets, look out! It was guaranteed to cause injury. I'm not kidding you when I say that every time I had to switch over to clean bedding, I somehow hurt myself. Stubbed toes on the base of the bed frame? You know it. Bent back fingernails on the tight sheet corners? Naturally. Knee knocking the sharp-cornered bedpost? Of course. Scraped knuckles on the adjacent wall? I'll show them to you right now if you want. I could go on. Did you even know there were so many ways to get hurt making a bed?

It wasn't just making the bed; it was also handling blankets. If the blanket needed folding, I was not your girl for the task (unless crooked edges are your thing). If I lay down on the couch, somehow my toes or elbows or shoulders would be uncovered—even if I used the biggest blanket of all. And sleeping overnight was the stuff of nightmares—and I'm not talking about actual bad dreams. I would pull the covers—even with that extra fabric I cheated with when I made it—and actually get tangled. It was laughable. And here we are, with me exposing my innermost struggles to the world. Go ahead, feel free to laugh. I know it's ridiculous, but hey, I'm owning it.

All joking aside, it's not a huge deal to be bad at something like bedding. Yes, my parents had me make my bed as a child. Yes, I'm a generally coordinated person. So really, I have no excuse. It's just something that doesn't quite work out for me, as much as I may try.

I have to give it to my husband, though. Andy would still encourage me to try my best to make the bed. Would he fix it after I inevitably messed it up? Yep, because he's a good husband and supports me "through better or worse" and bed-making difficulties. But also he encourages me to keep trying. Maybe I've even improved my skill level oh-so-slightly over the years.

Of course, it doesn't really matter to Andy whether I can make a good bed or not. Similarly, God knows we all have our strengths and weaknesses. What matters is that I keep trying, because I know it's the kindness of offering my time to do something, whether or not I may be good at it. And maybe that is what is most important: offering our gifts *and* working through our weaknesses to put kindness into action. And whether we're good or not-so-good at something, we can give thanks to God regardless.

Families

Have you ever wished you were good at something, but you couldn't quite get the hang of it? Maybe you have even been envious or jealous that someone you know is better than you at something. It can be hard for us to see someone who is good at something we struggle with.

Let's be honest: It can be hard to think kind thoughts about someone whom we feel jealous of, especially when we see them succeed at something that we want to be successful at. I remember when I was very young, one of my teachers (or parents maybe...?) told me that there would always be someone out there who was better than me. While that was humbling advice, it didn't soften the blow when someone beat me at something I wanted to be "the best" at.

The good news is, God loves us how we are. He knows we have certain talents and may have to work hard at some things in our lives. There may be things we never get that good at, no matter how hard we try. What's important is that we use our talents and gifts for God's purpose for our lives. It is also important that we share kindness towards others and celebrate the gifts they were given. Our jealousy can take a backseat to our kindness and thankfulness when we remember God's reminder to give thanks for everything in all circumstances.

Prayer

Lord God, please help me when I feel envious about other people's gifts and talents. Help me also to treat others with kindness instead of feeling jealousy toward them. Guide me to be kind and offer my gifts and talents to you and to others. Please also help me when I feel frustrated, when I want to be good at something that I struggle with. Help me to know that you are with me, and that I can be thankful in all circumstances. In your name, Amen.

Extension Activity

What is something you aren't great at and would like to be better at? Maybe it's making your bed. (That's mine!) Maybe it's helping out with something else around the house. Maybe it's drawing or painting, singing or dancing, a sport or activity. This week, take some time to work on that skill. If you still can't quite get the hang of it, that's okay! Tell God, thank You for giving you the chance to try it. If you get better at it, great! Give thanks to God for showing you how your work can pay off. Whatever happens, remember to thank God in the circumstance.

Kindness

Acts of kindness can make the biggest difference in someone's day.

Scripture

"Let us not become weary in doing good, for at the proper time we will reap a harvest if we do not give up. Therefore, as we have opportunity, let us do good to all people, especially to those who belong to the family of believers."

– GALATIANS 6:9–10

Parents

As a teacher, I am often very humbled by the kindness of my students. One of my students in my class this year brings me a daily token of appreciation. Every. Single. Day! Some days, it's a bag full of treats. (Today, in fact, she brought me a bag of Sour Patch Kids and Snickers, two of my top favorite treats!). Other days, it's a small craft or handpicked toy she made or found just for me. Most often, though, she will come into our classroom with a sweet card or note that tells me how much she loves me as her teacher.

Every day, I thank her for her thoughtfulness and kindness. Some days, I'll offer her a sticker to return my thanks (although now she's started gifting those right back to me!). Every day, regardless of how my morning has been going, I get a small act of kindness from a young child who is truly wiser than her years: she seems to understand that a small gesture of kindness can lift the spirits of the recipient. While I don't want to become expectant of her generosity, at this point I know to expect it and know that this sweet girl will brighten my day.

I appreciate this reminder that even the smallest acts of kindness can affect someone's day greatly. On those days when I need a pick-me-up, I get it from my thoughtful student. On those days that are already starting out pretty great, I get an even better day because of her. It has encouraged me to think of ways I can share kindness with others—much like the verse above encourages us to do!

Families

Have you ever been surprised by a friend or family member who has given you something when you didn't expect it? Maybe it was a thoughtful card, or a friendship bracelet, or an unexpected note just to say hi.

On the other hand, have you ever given someone something just because? Did you give something to your family or teacher or friend just to let them know you were thinking of them?

I am a teacher, and many of my students show their kindness to me with sweet notes or thoughtful gifts they make for me. Anytime one of my students shows me they're thinking of me, my heart smiles at the kindness they showed me. It reminds me to pass it on and share kindness with the people around me.

In the Bible verse today, we are reminded to do good things and not become weary or tired of doing them. Acts of kindness towards others are a really good way to share the love of Jesus with anyone we might see or know. When they see the kindness we are sharing, they can also see that we have God's love in our hearts because of the good things we choose to do for them.

Prayer

Heavenly Father, we are so thankful for all of the goodness and kindness we receive from you. Please help us to be good and kind to those around us. Help us to find ways to pass along kind and thoughtful notes, gifts, or words to the people we cross paths with, so that they can see you in our hearts. In your name we pray, Amen.

Extension Activity

Have you ever heard of Random Acts of Kindness? The idea behind it is to randomly do something kind for the recipient. It could be something small, like an anonymous note telling someone how wonderful they are. Or it could be something bigger, like paying for someone's fast food order behind you in the drive-through. Or it could be something creative, like painting pictures or knitting scarves and giving them to people to brighten their day. With your family, brainstorm ways you could do Random Acts of Kindness to people in your life or community. Maybe you can even think of a way to have the people on the receiving end of your kindness pass something kind along to others! See what you come up with, and try to share a few Random Acts of Kindness over the next week—or however long you can keep it going!

Kindness

Forgiveness is a way of showing kindness to others—and yourself.

Scripture

"Be kind and compassionate to one another, forgiving each other, just as in Christ God forgave you."

– EPHESIANS 4:32

Parents

I don't want to admit this, but I'm going to be raw in the hopes that it helps me (and maybe you) be real about a struggle: forgiveness seems to get harder the older I get.

Am I generally a kind person? Yes, but the honest part is that I have a hard time being kind and forgiving when someone has wronged me. Why is it so easy to hold a grudge against someone who has wronged me? I may even pretend to have forgiven them, but what they did just hangs out in the back of my mind for me to bring back up whenever I decide to.

Case in point: years ago, my husband was in a toxic work environment. Without going into much detail, the people who wronged him became the subject of many griping conversations. After a considerable amount of time, when some healing from that awful experience was able to happen, they became the butt of many of our unkind jokes.

The way my husband was treated... Well, let's just say, these people needed to be forgiven for what they did. So here lies the challenge the verse above presents: while I was defensive of the person I love the most in this world, I was also not forgiving the people I needed to, who severely wronged him.

Who, then, am I really punishing? My unforgiveness, while protective and supportive toward my husband in his toxic workplace situation, really only punishes me because I am holding onto those angry feelings, and maybe also punishing my husband because I'm not helping him get past it either.

While the Scripture above seems to have an uplifting tone at first, I encourage you to truly explore your heart. Maybe then we determine who we need to forgive, using Christ as our example. God has helped me work through these feelings to finally offer forgiveness to even the most difficult people to forgive, because He knows I can't do it without Him!

Families

Have you ever heard the phrase "Forgive and forget"? I hope you have an easier time doing this than I do! When someone has treated me badly, I have a very hard time forgiving them for what they did. If I can get to the point of forgiveness, I have an even harder time forgetting what they did to me.

This is something I know I have to do better at. I have asked God to help me work on forgiving people when I need to in my life. The Bible verse at the beginning of the chapter encourages us to forgive each other as a way to show kindness—even when it's not easy.

God has helped me realize, over the years, that when I hold a grudge of unforgiveness, it really only hurts my own heart. The other person who did something wrong may or may not have moved on with their life, but I am stuck in the past as long as I hold onto the thing that happened.

Both of my children are like their mom in this way. As a parent to kids who need to work on this, my husband and I have talked about ways to help them forgive people who have done something to upset them. (It's especially hard when their parents have the same tendencies!)

We know that people come from all different circumstances, and sometimes someone might act out toward us in a way that needs to be forgiven. Sometimes, our own friends and family treat us in a way that needs to be forgiven. Sometimes, people can be repeatedly unkind toward us. These can all be examples of people who need our forgiveness, as hard as it may be.

My husband and I remind our kids that, after we forgive those who have wronged us (and maybe continue to wrong us), we can do what is in our control to move past it. God can help us all along the way when these circumstances arise.

Prayer

Dear Heavenly Father, there are some times in our lives when we have a hard time forgiving what someone has done to us. Sometimes it is a friend or family member who has hurt us; other times it's someone who repeatedly tears us down. Even though what they're doing may be wrong, when we find ourselves in these circumstances, please help us to lean on you to forgive them for their actions, just as Jesus forgives us. Thank you for giving us your Son to offer us forgiveness for all of our sins, and help us to be more like Him. In Your name we pray, Amen.

Extension Activity

Is there anyone in your life you need to forgive? We are going to take some time working through forgiving those people who have been a challenge to forgive. Maybe something happened recently, or maybe it's been years. Take some time to reflect on who you might need to forgive. Then, write a letter or note or draw a picture that tells or shows that you forgive them. Pray about whether you should actually give that person the letter or note to offer them your forgiveness. If God leads you to give that person your note, follow His guidance. Maybe writing this letter is more of a way for you to process what you've been through; if so, decide if you need to throw it away, keep it in a drawer, safely burn it (of course with adult supervision!), etc. As you work through this process, keep a prayerful approach to allow God to help you forgive that person.

Then, since this activity might feel pretty heavy, let's also add in a little fun: play the classic board game Sorry! with your family! You might be familiar with the game: you move your pieces around the board and occasionally have to say "Sorry!" for sending other players' pieces back to the start. As you play, have fun forgiving others as they tell you "Sorry!" and they can do the same for you!

Kindness

Look at others with kindness.

Scripture

"Jacob said, 'If I have found favor in your eyes, accept this gift from me. For to see your face is like seeing the face of God, now that you have received me favorably. Please accept the present that was brought to you, for God has been gracious to me and I have all I need.' And because Jacob insisted, Esau accepted it."

– GENESIS 33:10-11

Parents

This Scripture invites us into a beautiful story of forgiveness and extravagant kindness. For some background, Jacob had deceitfully stolen his brother's birthright and blessing, leaving Esau, who was intended to receive it, with no blessing. Instead, he was commissioned to live away from richness and to serve under his brother.

Initially, caught up in anger and distress of being tricked, Esau plots to murder Jacob out of spite and a heart burning with revenge. However, six chapters later and after some time had passed, we find this Scripture describing their reunion. Jacob sent ahead gifts for Esau in an attempt to ease the tension and prayed that God would treat him kindly, despite him being undeserving. Jacob is relieved and grateful that his brother accepts him, as we see him describe seeing Esau's face to be like seeing the face of God.

It had to have taken a lot of kindness and humility on Esau's part to forgive his brother and accept him back genuinely and lovingly, after the ultimate deception. In response to that lavish kindness, we see Jacob feeling that, through Esau, he experienced God himself.

Have you ever experienced a kindness so extravagant or unexpected that you felt God shining through? I know, even in my marriage, when I mess up or communicate unkindly, I feel like I see God through my husband when his response to my behavior is kind and patient. Kindness always, but especially when undeserved, can feel like a glimpse of heaven and leaves me with extreme gratitude.

I love this Scripture and the idea of viewing others with kindness and, in turn, seeing the face of God. Knowing we are all created in God's image, it is beautiful to think about seeing them truly and purely as a child of God—not as the mistake they made, an annoying characteristic, or a difference in viewpoints.

I think about my children, Jack and Emmy, and how when I look at them, all I see is absolute awe, wonder, and love. Do I get frustrated when they wake up for the 25th time that night, or when they say no when I ask them to do something? Absolutely! But I couldn't love them more if I tried because they are my children. In the ultimate form of kindness, God looks at us with the same kind, loving, forgiving eyes, seeing us as His beloved children.

How can we extend forgiveness and kindness to others today? Will others be able to see the face of God in us through our actions? Can we ask God to help us view others as His children today?

Families

Later in this devotional, you will read about one of my favorite books of all time: *Wonder!* It will be described in more detail in the goodness section, but it is an amazing story about viewing others with wonder, treating them with kindness, and the difference it can make when you do so!

One of my favorite quotes from the book is "Look with kindness and you will always find wonder." I have it posted on my classroom door because it is such a great reminder to begin each day afresh, viewing others through a lens of kindness and understanding. When we choose to see people in a kind light rather than in a judgmental way, we can begin to appreciate the wonders that they are and see how God created them: fearfully, wonderfully, and uniquely.

Before you step outside today, put on your kindness glasses. Envision yourself wearing them all day! What wonders can you appreciate in others when you look at them with kindness?!

Prayer

Dear God, thank you for creating us and others with unique qualities, passions, and characteristics. Give us kind eyes to see the goodness in others. Please fill us with kindness so that when they see and interact with us, they see and experience you. In Jesus' name, Amen.

Extension Activity

The theme of my classroom is *Wonder,* and something that we have and add to all year long is a "kindness chain." Each time I catch students being kind, I add their name to the chain, and we see how long it can get! Midway through the year I allow them to be kindness finders, and they can also add others' names to the chain!

Your challenge this week is to create your own kindness chain! Cut links of paper, and each time you catch someone in your family being kind, add their name to the chain! See how long you can make it by the end of the week!

Kindness

You may never know who needs to receive kindness from you.

Scripture

"Gracious words are a honeycomb, sweet to the soul and healing to the bones."

– PROVERBS 16:24

Parents

One of the most challenging and mentally taxing experiences of my life was giving birth. I've persevered through some difficult times and even gotten through a marathon, but enduring the pain and exhaustion of childbirth was unlike any other difficulty I had experienced to date!

Right before Jack was born, we found out that the doctor who saw us for our prenatal appointments, whom I loved and trusted, did not have privileges to deliver our baby at the new hospital. I was upset and worried, facing so many unknowns. I had never gone through this before, but I had found peace in at least knowing who would be in the room. With that now being out of my control, my husband and I prayed that we would be given a doctor who respected our wishes and that we would feel His presence in the delivery room.

During my birth experience, the doctor who was on call, although capable and talented in many ways and very respectful and honoring of our birth plan, did not have very good bedside manner. She was dry and short and only checked in periodically. In addition, she refused to check me throughout the day to see how dilated I was, saying that it wouldn't matter anyway, as I had hoped for an unmedicated birth. At one point, she even told me that my birth could last an additional twenty-four hours and that I wasn't very far along—not what you want to hear after eighteen hours of contractions and labor!

At that point, I was feeling defeated, unseen, and discouraged. How could I last much longer—I was exhausted! I remember just praying for intervention and progress and that God would help me because I had nothing left to give.

After enduring about twenty hours of labor, a new shift of nurses came, and my mom and husband explained our situation. Immediately, they checked me and found that I was eight centimeters dilated! I was so encouraged—it wouldn't be much longer. I could do this!

Where the doctor lacked encouragement, the nurses were kind and present, affirming that I was strong and capable and could do this. With them, my mom, and my husband by my side, I felt a new charge of motivation and energy. Their kind words carried and motivated me, and a couple of hours later, our son was born.

My husband and I have both taken the love language test. (If you haven't taken it yourself, check it out—there are several available online, and it's worth discovering how you best give and receive love.) I always knew that words of affirmation meant the most to me, but I never realized to what extent until I needed them the most. Words have power, and I am certain that God was present in the delivery room in many ways, but especially through the kindness and encouragement of the people surrounding me that day. As the proverb says, kind words truly are like honey.

Families

One of my favorite picture books to read and teach about kindness is *The Invisible Boy,* by Trudy Ludwig (check it out this week if you're not familiar with it!). It is a story about a boy who feels alone and invisible until a new boy, Justin, moves into school and treats him with kindness. Justin offers the boy who feels invisible small acts of kindness and encouraging words that make him feel noticed and visible, and give him the strength to shine.

Just like Justin, we have the capability to make people feel visible, included, and seen. However, we also have the power to make others feel invisible, excluded, and unseen. Our words and actions can make others feel loved and encouraged. In the same breath, they can make others feel unloved and discouraged.

What will you choose today? Will your words be like honey and add sweetness to the people who are with you today? Or will your words be like poison and make others feel hurt and sad?

Prayer

Dear God, thank you for the gift of words. We know our words can be used to build up or destroy, and we pray that you use ours today to encourage those around us. Speak through us today, and may our words be "like honey—sweet to the soul and healthy for the body." In Jesus' name, Amen.

Extension Activity

Take a fresh piece of paper and crumple it up into a tight ball. Smash it, step on it, and make it as small of a ball as possible!

Now, carefully, without ripping it, uncrumple it and try to make it smooth again. Can you get all the crinkles out and make it look like it was before? Similarly, when we say something unkind, it never goes away. Our words make a mark on others and leave an imprint.

With your family, have everyone take a piece of paper and write your name in the center (don't crumple this one!). Pass the paper around the circle and write one kind note on the page describing the person whose name you see (or draw a picture to show what you appreciate about them!). Pass the papers around until you get yours back. How did it feel to speak kind words to others? How did it feel to have others encourage you?

Goodness

Grapes are the fruit we chose to represent *Goodness*. First of all, they both start with the letter G, so that was a minor connection worth noting. More importantly, though, purple grapes are also the color of royalty. We are all princes and princesses of God, as children of the King. We can do so much good for the Kingdom of God—what could be "more good" than grapes?!

Goodness is

Great!
(or should i say... GRAPE!)

Goodness

There is *always* something to be grateful for.

Scripture

"Finally, brothers and sisters, whatever is true, whatever is noble, whatever is right, whatever is pure, whatever is lovely, whatever is admirable—if anything is excellent or praiseworthy—think about such things."

– PHILIPPIANS 4:8

Parents

When I graduated from college, I was given a gratitude journal. Based on Ann Voskamp's book *1,000 Gifts* (check it out!), the devotional and notebook were designed to help you seek God's gifts surrounding you, not just in the extraordinary events but also in the quiet, ordinary moments that make up our day-to-day lives. However, in the busyness of post-college adjustments to the real world, I put the journal aside and didn't open it for a couple of years.

After graduating, I had a really hard time! I was starting a new teaching job, planning a wedding, in grad school, and buying a house all at once (why not go big or go home!), and found myself consumed by the stress of it all. I've always been a perfectionist and have had a fear of failure for as long as I can remember, but I found myself struggling with this even more as I got my own classroom and everything was new. I had a lot of anxiety and put so much pressure on myself to succeed. On top of that, the community of friends that I had been blessed with in high school and college was stripped away, and I found myself feeling anxious and alone. Rather than seeing the gifts surrounding me, all I could focus on and think about was how I was not measuring up, or failing, compared to the veteran teachers around me. Through those years of stress and anxiety, it was easy to focus on scarcity (what was lacking) rather than the abundance a life with Christ offers.

Every January, I love to make New Year's resolutions, and so in January 2017 (during my third year of teaching), I made it my goal that year to write down one thing each day that I had been grateful for! It was a simple task, but as the days, weeks, and months went on, I found my mind looking for good things that happened each day. Rather than meditating on anxious thoughts, I found God slowly but surely helping me to see His presence in the midst of it all.

I am now on day 3,195 (and counting) of writing in my gratitude journal. What started as a New Year's resolution has turned into a daily practice that has transformed my outlook and grounds me. Looking back on the past entries, it is amazing to reflect on God's goodness. These past 3,194 days have had a lot of amazing highs (getting our rambunctious Goldendoodle Copper, traveling to countries around the world, special time with family and friends, the births of our beautiful children Jack and Emmy, and pumpkin spice lattes :)), but they have also held a lot of lows (losing grandparents and people that I love, watching loved ones hurt, and frustrating and scary moments in my community, country, and the world).

However, through this practice of gratitude, I am reminded of Paul's words that as we focus on what is true, noble, right, pure, lovely, admirable, excellent, and praiseworthy, we can be reassured that God is "working together all things for the good of those who love Him." (Romans 8). Life may not be perfect, and it is most definitely hard at times. Although our circumstances may not alter, by changing our mindset and choosing what we meditate on, God can flood our hearts with his love, grace, peace, and goodness, in an abundance found only in Him.

Families

One of my absolute favorite holidays is Thanksgiving! What are some of your favorite Thanksgiving treats? Maybe your family is like mine and makes some amazing foods on that day. Between the turkey, stuffing, mashed potatoes, and pumpkin pie, I look forward to that meal and feast every year!

Another tradition my family has at Thanksgiving time is going around the table and saying something we are grateful for that year. It is always fun to hear from everyone what has been a blessing to them.

Whether it is a family member, teacher, friend, pet, stuffed animal, favorite trip, event, or activity, God has given us so much to be thankful for! Although it may not be Thanksgiving when you are reading this, take some time today to reflect upon some people or things God has blessed you with. I bet you will be amazed by the list you can see!

Prayer

God, thank you so much for the goodness that you offer. You have given us so many blessings, beyond what we could ever ask for or imagine. Help us to remember that even when times are hard, you are with us and working all things together for our good. Give us eyes to see and seek your blessings in the midst of our daily lives. Amen.

Extension Activity

Grab a piece of paper and your favorite markers, crayons (or if you're like me—sparkly gel pens!). Set your timer for ten minutes and create a Gratitude Explosion!

Write down or draw for ten minutes as many things as you can think of that you are grateful for: people, food, pets, events—absolutely anything! Nothing is too big or too small to name. :) After the ten minutes are up, share your gratitude explosions with one another. I think you will be surprised and amazed at how much there is to be grateful for and how full of goodness your life really is. :)

Goodness

God's goodness shines through His steadfast love and can be seen at work through the people, events, and surroundings of our lives.

Scripture

"Surely your goodness and love will follow me all the days of my life, and I will dwell in the house of the LORD forever."

– PSALM 23:6

"Every good and perfect gift is from above, coming down from the Father of the heavenly lights, who does not change like shifting shadows."

– 1 CHRONICLES 16:11

Parents

While I was in college, I started running. It was a chance for me to clear my mind and take a break from whatever I was working on and doing. In my senior year of college, I ran my first half-marathon in Pittsburgh and totally fell in love with it.

Let's be clear—I didn't totally fall in love with the sore muscles, how I could barely walk up the stairs the next day, the mental game of 13.1 miles, or the measly banana that they gave you when you crossed the finish line (I **still** won't understand why a banana is considered a sufficient reward for the agony you just put your body through!).

Rather than that, I fell in love with the community of it all. Although an individual race, the spectators cheering on total strangers, being surrounded by people of all walks of life walking or running on towards the same goal, bands serenading you with music to pump you up, volunteers lining up to give you water, and Panera Bread bagels and chocolate milk at the end were a few of the perks that made the day absolutely amazing and awe-inspiring.

After I graduated from college, I joined a running group and was blessed with a group of women who were dedicated to running or walking every Tuesday, Thursday, and Sunday, rain, shine, or snow. They made each three-mile, 5:30 a.m. run fly by, as you were never at a loss for a good talk, sunrise, laugh, or pause to take a selfie along the way. It was all about the journey and good company to share it with.

So, being spoiled by always having someone by my side, I was caught off guard a couple of years ago when I began another 13.1-mile adventure totally alone! Nobody else had signed up for the race, and so it was just me. How was I supposed to get through this by myself without someone distracting me?

By the time I reached the midway point of the run, my brain was in need of something to get me through the final home stretch. With no person to talk to, I decided to talk to God. For each mile that followed, I decided to talk with God about something. Each mile had a theme. At first, it was prayer requests, but then I decided, for the next mile, to share with God things I was grateful for. It soon became apparent that one mile wasn't enough! I could spend a whole mile just meditating on people I was grateful for, another two on events in my life, another on examples of God's faithfulness, and another on things that brought me **joy**. It was amazing to realize just how much God had blessed me. Even things I once viewed as hardships—it was encouraging to see how God had used them as gifts for good.

If you're having a hard time seeing the good in life (we all have days where it's harder than others), I encourage you today to set your timer for ten minutes, or set an intention on your drive to work, and meditate solely on things for which you are grateful to God. If your mind wanders, it's okay! Acknowledge it, and just bring your thoughts back to evidence of His goodness.

Families

Have you ever been given a gift that you loved?! Maybe at Christmas time or on your birthday? I remember one of my favorite gifts that I received growing up was an American Girl doll. I **loved** getting special outfits for her to dress her up in and reading books about her life. It also meant so much to me that my parents thought of me and got her for me.

As fun as it is to receive gifts, it is even more fun to give gifts! There is nothing I enjoy more than finding the **perfect** gift for a friend or family member that I know they will love.

Just as we enjoy giving and receiving gifts, our Father in Heaven **loves** to shower us with gifts. Whether it is in the form of a beautiful sunset when we are out for a walk, a rainbow painted across the sky after a storm, laughter at something that brightened your day, friendships that bring goodness to your life, a loving word from a family member, the presence of a pet, or promises of love in His Word, God loves to show you how much He loves you! Go out in the world today with your eyes wide open for what God is trying to bless you with today.

Prayer

God, thank you so much for the many gifts you give us, and the many ways you speak to us. Through nature, through your people, through your word, you are constantly communicating to us your extravagant love for us. Please help us to keep our eyes, ears, and hearts open for what you are giving us and speaking to us today. We love you, Lord. Amen.

Extension Activity

Who is ready for a scavenger hunt? *Woo!* I am **pumped!** Today, you are not just going on any old scavenger hunt. No, you are going on a scavenger hunt for God's goodness. Go out in nature or outside and find some of the many gifts God created for you to enjoy! Whether it's animals, a cotton-candy-colored sky, bright green grass, tall trees, a cool breeze, ants crawling on your feet, or light raindrops falling on your face, keep your body attuned for God's presence and beautiful creation surrounding you! Then share with your family members what stood out to you! Finally, thank God for the many gifts He has given you.

Goodness

Do good! God will bless you with glory, honor, and peace.

Scripture

"There will be trouble and distress for every human being who does evil: first for the Jew, then for the Gentile; but glory, honor, and peace for everyone who does good: first for the Jew, then for the Gentile. For God does not show favoritism."

– ROMANS 2:9–11

Parents

As adults, my three siblings and I drive my wonderful parents crazy by joking about who their "favorite" child is. We didn't dare joke like that when we were younger, because they made it very clear that they could never pick a favorite. So now we make up for that lost time: We tease my older sister, Melissa, and say she is their favorite because she gave my parents the most grandbabies, not to mention she is the kindest soul ever. Sometimes we jokingly crown ourselves the "favorite" when we've had an especially thoughtful moment, like the time I wrote 48 reasons my mom is wonderful on each of the 48 K-Cups in a pack I gave her as a gift.

Our spouses have gotten in on the joke. They will egg us on, and sometimes they'll even try to "earn" the "favorite child" title themselves. At one point, we even had full rankings from top to bottom, declaring who was the favorite of all the adult kids and their spouses, as well as the least favorite, and everything in between. My parents are always very good-natured about it, but we know it bothers them a little because they would never have a favorite child.

The book of Romans simultaneously keeps me in check while also reminding me how much God loves me. This particular verse (above) reminds me that, no matter what my background, God doesn't have favorites (hence, keeping me in check). This verse also gives me a much-needed reminder that glory, honor, and peace come to me if I do good (you got it: a reminder of how much God loves me). I also love that this verse reminds me that my goodness isn't based on God's favoritism towards me. God doesn't rank us as "most good" or "least good" or anything in between. God doesn't choose favorites based on things, like who writes the most K-Cup compliments. (Listen, I'd totally win that one.) True, He rewards us with glory, honor, and peace when we do good. But it's good to know that He's not showing favoritism based on whether we're a "Jew" or "Gentile" or whatever our background, even when we ourselves are trying to keep track of "how good" we might be.

Families

When I was in elementary school, I had one teacher who always called on the same kid. She asked that student to run errands to the office for her, to help with classroom chores, to answer the questions during all of our lessons. If you've ever heard the term "teacher's pet"... well, that was this student.

It was very obvious to me, and everyone else in my class, that this student was the teacher's pet, or the teacher's favorite student. In my teacher's eyes, this child could do no wrong. In fact, that student was the *perfect* student, in my teacher's opinion. It really bothered me because it was very clear that I was *not* the favorite student. It was hard not to be shown favoritism when someone else was so clearly receiving it. (As a teacher now, I realize that this child may have needed some extra love. And I believe the teacher may have been showing extra love by giving that student extra compliments and privileges. And I wonder if maybe I didn't see the whole story. But to my point here, it still didn't make it easy to see favoritism shown toward someone else and not toward me.)

In the verse above from Romans, we read that God doesn't show favoritism. That means God doesn't choose favorites. God loves all of His children. He loves His children who live in cities or in the country. He loves His children whether they are rich or poor. He loves His children who are funny or clumsy or thoughtful or smart or ___________ (insert a word that would describe **you** on that line). That's right! God loves all of us, and He doesn't pick favorites!

Isn't it wonderful to know that God doesn't pick favorites? What He *does* promise all of His children is that when we do good, we will be rewarded with glory, honor, and peace. So in my elementary classroom years ago, where that one student was constantly rewarded, it was based on the teacher's favoritism. But our reward for the goodness we do comes from God. And that sounds like a great reward to me!

Prayer

Lord God, we are so grateful that you don't have favorites. Thank you for Your love, no matter where we are coming from. Thank you for the reminder that doing good in your name will reward us with glory, honor, and peace. Help us to remember to do as much good as we can so that we can bring that glory, honor, and peace to your name. It's in your holy name that we pray, Amen.

Extension Activity

Siren blares Goodness Patrol coming through! Yes, that's you!

It's time to catch people being good. In our lives, we often see the bad things that happen and think of those things. This activity is to open your eyes to the good happening around you.

Get a notebook, sticky notes, or slips of paper. Or maybe you want to go the extra mile and print off "Caught You Being Good!" certificates! Carry your choice of reward papers with you throughout the rest of the day (or all day tomorrow). When you catch someone doing good, write down what you saw. Then give it to that person as a reward from the Goodness Patrol!

It might also be fun to hand a *blank* "Caught You Being Good" certificate with each filled-out one you hand to an unsuspecting do-gooder. That way, they can pay it forward and find someone else being good. Who knows, this whole goodness thing might really catch on!

Goodness

Seek the good of others and many
as you follow Jesus's example.

Scripture

"'I have the right to do anything,' you say, but not everything is beneficial. I have the right to do anything, but not everything is constructive. No one should seek their own good, but the good of others... So whether you eat or drink or whatever you do, do it all for the glory of God. Do not cause anyone to stumble, whether Jews, Greeks, or the church of God—even as I try to please everyone in every way. For I am not seeking my own good but the good of many, so that they may be saved. Follow my example, as I follow the example of Christ."

– 1 CORINTHIANS 10:23-24;10:31-11:1

Parents

Every year for quite a few years now, I read a fictitious book called *Wonder* as well as its companion book, *Auggie & Me,* by R.J. Palacio, to my third graders. If you haven't read these books, I highly recommend them for children of all ages! (Okay, maybe not much younger than third grade, but definitely most ages.)

The storyline follows a boy named Auggie, who has something called "mandibulofacial dysostosis"—which basically means the development of his bones and other facial tissues is severely affected.

Auggie looks very different from all other people. His story is both heart-wrenching and heartwarming as it follows the trials he experiences.

Throughout the story, I'm always impacted by the choices of the people around Auggie. Without spoiling much (like I said, you should probably go read these books now if you haven't already... it's fine, I'll be here when you're back)... Okay, great! Where was I? Oh, right. Like I was going to say, I'm drawn to the people in Auggie's life who treat him in a good, kind way.

I'm also hurt on behalf of Auggie by the people who treat him badly. However, when we look more closely at the different characters' stories, there's always more than meets the eye. The characters who treat Auggie badly have also experienced trials in their own ways. While their actions aren't necessarily justified, there is a reason why they are the way they are. Isn't that true of life? We have no idea what someone's journey has brought them through. We may have a glimpse, or even a pretty good idea, but humans are complex.

In the complexity that is humanity, however, we should keep the verse above in mind that tells us, "No one should seek their own good, but the good of others."

Wow. Well, that one is a bit counterintuitive, isn't it? It's in our nature to protect ourselves and our families, and often that might mean we seek our own good at the expense of pursuing the good of others.

In Auggie's stories, I remember the people in Auggie's life who are self-seeking, and it saddens me. But it also reminds me that I can be like that sometimes, too. I am also always so touched by Auggie's numerous school supervisors, friends, and people who come into his life who look out for him, who have his back no matter what. They put Auggie first instead of themselves. When we do these same things in a Christian way, as the Scripture above reminds us, we can *follow* the example of Christ and be the example of Christ for those around us.

Families

There is a fantastic children's book for young kids called *We're All Wonders* by R.J. Palacio. You might want to read it, if you can! (There is another set of books for older kids called *Wonder* and *Auggie & Me*. These are such great books to read, too!)

These books all tell a story about a boy who looks different from other kids. Even though he looks different, he loves to do things that other kids do.

God created us all to be different. Can you imagine a world in which we were all the same? **Bor-ing!** But sometimes seeing things that are different can make us feel uncomfortable. We might not know the right way to act or the good, kind thing to do.

The Bible passage above reminds us that, "Whatever you do, do it all for the glory of God." That means we should treat others well and lovingly, because that is the example set for us by Jesus. It shouldn't matter if someone looks like a regular, everyday kid, or if they have hair made of gummy worms! (That sounds super fun, actually!) We should all remember to "seek the good of others," as these verses say.

In the book, *We're All Wonders,* the narrator reminds the reader to "look with kindness." (I guess this devotion could also qualify for the "Kindness" Fruit of the Spirit section, too! Consider this a little bit of what we like to call "Fruit Salad!") When we can see each other and "seek the good of others," as this passage says, we can treat others in a way that they can see Jesus' example. It's so important to treat people—all people—with goodness, no matter what they may do or look like.

Prayer

Heavenly Father, we ask you to be with the people in our lives who might not see your goodness around them. We pray that you will help us to be the ones who seek their good so that they can see the example you have shown us in our lives. In your holy name, Amen.

Extension Activity

Years ago, in Sunday School or Vacation Bible School or church camp, I learned a valuable lesson of putting God first, others second, and ourselves third. In this Extension Activity, we will be making a poster to remind us to do those same things.

You'll need a piece of paper, a digital document, a posterboard, or whatever you decide to create this visual reminder on. Then, do what my teacher or counselor told me to do: write down the numbers 1, 2, and 3 *really* big. I wrote them going up and down the left-hand column of my page. Next to the big number 1, write *"God."* By the number 2, write *"Others."* And by the number 3, write *"Me."* Then design and decorate your poster in whatever way you want—use your creativity!

Use this visual as a reminder to seek God's wisdom first by coming to Him in prayer and reading the Bible. Secondly, as the Scripture for this lesson reminds us, seek the good of others and be a good friend to them. And then, when we get to ourselves third, we can know that we have followed God's directions for us!

Goodness

Thank God for His boundless love, grace, and endless blessings!

Scripture

"Let them give thanks to the Lord for his unfailing love and his wonderful deeds for mankind, for he satisfies the thirsty and fills the hungry with good things."

– PSALM 107:8–9

"The Lord loves righteousness and justice; the earth is full of the unfailing love of the Lord."

– PSALM 33:5

Parents

When I was younger, one of my favorite books and movies was *The Sisterhood of the Traveling Pants* by Ann Brashares. In one of the most tender scenes in the first movie, a little girl named Bailey, who was battling cancer, shared some wisdom with one of the main characters during her final days. She said, "Being happy isn't having everything in your life be perfect. Maybe it's about stringing together all the little things, like wearing these pants or getting to a new level of Dragon's Lair—making those count for more than the bad stuff."

Seven years ago, I experienced my first death of someone who was close to me. My grandma was suddenly diagnosed with cancer, and months after her diagnosis, she passed away. Growing up in the same town as both sets of my grandparents and getting to spend a lot of time with them was one of the greatest blessings in my life, so it was really hard watching her decline and grappling with her no longer being with us.

I had the honor of speaking at her funeral, which, although hard, was a great way for me to process who she was and the impact that she had on my life. She had left a list of a few things that she wanted in her funeral before she passed away: special hymns that she loved, people she wanted to be a part of it, and a favorite poem titled "Little Things." The poem is written on the next page:

Little Things
By Myrtle E. Shafer

A smile is such a little thing,
as is a word of praise,
but each of them can warm a heart
and make a happy day.

A helping hand,
a kindly deed,
or just a friendly wave
could lighten someone's burden,
could fill another need.

These are all just little things
as we go along our way,
but little things are big things
if they brighten someone's day.

Reading this poem totally embodied my grandma. Her life was filled with little acts of goodness. She lived a quiet, simple life but with big love. Her goodness will be remembered by me in the way she brought a jar of pears she had canned herself when she found out one of us wasn't feeling well, the way she collected items to pack shoe boxes each Christmas for Operation Christmas Child, her sugar cookies and how she brought extra just for me when discovering my dad and brother ate them all, the way she tended to her garden and flowers, and how she loved to play games and spend time together. She knew and lived out that goodness isn't only in the big things but rather can be felt in the consistent, daily discoveries of the little things.

I think God's goodness is similar. Not only does He love to bless us in big, extravagant ways, but I think He also loves to plant little reminders of His goodness along our path, just waiting to be discovered, like in the sunrise on our way to work, the smile of a familiar face when we feel alone, and the playing of our favorite worship song when we're doubting He's there. His goodness is everywhere, just waiting to be discovered, and He desires nothing more than to fill our longing hearts with it.

Families

Have you ever made or eaten Chex Mix? At Christmas time, there are a couple of families who always make us homemade Chex Mix, and it is soooooo good (my mouth is watering right now just thinking about it!). Part of what makes Chex Mix so great is that each individual component is so good—the peanuts, the Chex pieces, the pretzels, the brown crunchy pieces (my personal favorite), the breadsticks, the Cheez-its (or whatever your variety has)—but together, it is truly something delicious! Even if you don't like every part, it is still yummy when combined, and there is still goodness to be found in each bag.

God's goodness reminds me a lot of a bag of Chex Mix. It is found everywhere and in every part (even in the hard and not-so-great parts). Some parts you may like more than others, but in each bag or moment, His goodness is there—waiting to be noticed and experienced. His goodness is made up of all of the little things, just as much as it is found in His greatest gift of all, His Son dying on the cross so that we can experience eternal life with Him. Be on the lookout today for the little ways you see God—He wants nothing more than to fill you with His love.

Prayer

Dear God, thank you for all of the little ways you appear to us and that your goodness is everywhere, just waiting to be found. You are so good and so creative, and we praise you for all of the ways you've filled the Earth with your goodness, and for filling our hungry souls, as well, in a way that only you can satisfy. We love you, Lord, and praise you for who you are. In Jesus' name, Amen.

Extension Activity

You can probably guess what this week's activity will involve... Chex Mix! Yay! Look up your favorite recipe (or select your own favorite ingredients) and mix them all together for a snack this week! As you create, eat, and enjoy, reflect on the little ways you have noticed God around you and little examples of His goodness in your life! I bet you will be able to list more ways than the number of ingredients in your yummy snack!

Goodness

In our weakness, God's Spirit guides and works all things for good.

Scripture

"In the same way, the Spirit helps us in our weakness. We do not know what we ought to pray for, but the Spirit himself intercedes for us through wordless groans. And he who searches our hearts knows the mind of the Spirit, because the Spirit intercedes for God's people in accordance with the will of God. And we know that in all things God works for the good of those who love him, who have been called according to his purpose."

– ROMANS 8:26-28

Parents

Have you ever had a day when you just felt totally overwhelmed?! Today I was trying to pack for my nineteen-month-old and me to head to Disney. I had gotten little sleep because our sweet boy was up most of the night with a cold and loves to sleep **very** closely to us, horizontally, so you're gifted either with his head or feet. Jack loves to help me pack by removing everything I put in the suitcase and hiding it in a cool spot (he's so talented!), so everything was taking twice as long. Simultaneously, I was trying to finish some things for my dad's surprise gift for his birthday, clean up the house so it was ready for our dog sitter, and get all of the dishes and laundry done so I could finish packing. I didn't even know how to ask my husband, Josh, for help because there were so many things that needed to be done!

One year during teaching, I felt so overwhelmed. I had a lot of students with significant needs, and there was little support and time in my schedule to get things done that were needed. It was a particularly challenging year, and I was bringing a lot of the stress home. On top of that, it was my first year back from maternity leave, so I was navigating being a working mom for the first time. It was really wearing on me, and I felt like I wasn't doing any one thing well. I was merely surviving—definitely not thriving—on all accounts!

I had read this Scripture before and rediscovered it during the year. I would read it and reread it, and it gave me so much comfort knowing that even when I felt that I couldn't do it or didn't even know where to start or what to pray for, that God did. He knew my heart so well that His Spirit would intercede on my behalf. How cool is it that the creator of the universe knows what we need before we even do? And that He can work hard situations or seasons into something good and beautiful on our behalf?

That year was the hardest to date, but I truly feel that God, in all of His goodness, interceded for me and shone through me in a way that I hadn't allowed Him to before. I quickly learned that I couldn't do it on my own, and by surrendering to Him and depending on Him, He was able to accomplish far more than I ever could have.

He also taught me humility in learning that it was okay to ask for help. Allowing myself to rely on Him and others was such a gift and was a lesson I needed to learn. It truly takes a village, and I was so grateful that God's goodness and provision carried me when I finally allowed Him to take control rather than independently and pridefully trying to do it all.

So if you're feeling overwhelmed and you don't know where to begin, ask His Spirit to intervene on your behalf. You'll be amazed at how God will use it (and you) for His good when you lay it at His feet.

Families

Close your eyes and imagine that you are stranded on a deserted island. You are **sooo** hungry, but there are no McDonald's or Wendy's. In fact, there is no food to be found!

Then all of a sudden, out of nowhere, a plane comes. After landing, the doors swing open, and down comes a chef delivering your all-time favorite meal. (For me, it would be a Chick-fil-A #1 meal with Chick-fil-A sauce, half iced tea, half lemonade, or homemade kabobs, pasta salad, and corn on the cob.) How would you feel?! Is your mouth watering just thinking about it?

Open your eyes and think about how amazing that would be! You didn't even have to ask for it, but the chef knew exactly what you needed and wanted!

Similarly, God knows exactly what we need before we even have to ask. He knows our hearts and minds, and if we feel stressed or overwhelmed, He knows exactly what will help us. We know we can always go to God and pray when we need His help, but even if you don't know what to pray for, His Spirit will hop in and know what you need. He is ready to work all of our hard, deserted island situations into something good and beautiful, so take comfort knowing today that God is with you and working for your good even when you can't feel it!

Prayer

Dear God, thank you for the amazing gift of your Spirit and the assurance that you are always with us. Even when we have hard days or feel totally stressed, you are there, working all things together for our good. Help us to rest in that comfort today, knowing we are exactly where we are meant to be, and that we are not alone. In Jesus' name, Amen.

Extension Activity

Grab a big jar. Also, grab larger rocks that will fit in the jar (or balls or whatever you have on hand), small pebbles, and some sand.

Round 1: Fill the jar first with the sand, then the pebbles, then the rocks/balls. Observe how comfortably everything fits inside and how much room is left in the jar.

Round 2: This time, fill the jar first with the big rocks/balls, then the pebbles, and finally the sand. Observe how comfortably everything fits inside and how much room is left in the jar.

If the experiment went correctly, you should have found that in round 2, everything fit in much more comfortably than in the first round! (If not, you can pretend! Haha.)

Just like how we need to put the big items in the jar first for everything to fit, in life, we need to put God first. If we start by trying to do all of the little things and put them in first, everything gets jumbled, and it's hard to squeeze it all in. However, when we prioritize Him and go to Him first, all of the other little details of our life will fall into place. His Spirit will help us sort out what really matters and work it all into the jar neatly, for our good. How can you put God first today?

Faithfulness

For *Faithfulness,* we chose the smallest fruit of our bunch: the *Blueberry!* We read in the Bible that you can have faith the size of a mustard seed, so the smallness of the blueberry is a reminder that with just a little faith, God can do great things.

Faithfulness is Amazing!!

Faithfulness

God's power exceeds all expectations;
He gives us more than we seek.

Scripture

"One day, Peter and John were going up to the temple at the time of prayer, at three in the afternoon. Now, a man who was lame from birth was being carried to the temple gate called Beautiful, where he was put every day to beg from those going into the temple courts. When he saw Peter and John about to enter, he asked them for money.

Peter looked straight at him, as did John. Then Peter said, 'Look at us!' So the man gave them his attention, expecting to get something from them.

Then Peter said, 'Silver or gold I do not have, but what I do have I give you. In the name of Jesus Christ of Nazareth, walk.' Taking him by the right hand, he helped him up, and instantly the man's feet and ankles became strong. He jumped to his feet and began to walk.

Then he went with them into the temple courts, walking and jumping and praising God. When all the people saw him walking and praising God, they recognized him as the same man who used to sit begging at the temple gate called Beautiful, and they were filled with wonder and amazement at what had happened to him."

– ACTS 3:1-10

Parents

My husband has a wonderful coffee mug (okay, I gifted it to him, so I'm a little biased). It's black with big, gold writing that says:

"I got this.
– God"

I gave it to Andy when he was going through an especially challenging time in his life, and rightfully so. There were so many things that were hurting him, and it had taken a huge toll on him.

Sometimes it's easy to get caught up in a self-pity party, especially when things around you are hurting your heart. When it hasn't been your day, or week, or month, or even your year (yes, I'm also singing the theme song to *Friends* now), we can easily turn to a "woe is me" mentality. I've been there.

The year that I'm writing this is 2020. Maybe that's self-explanatory, but if you need a reminder, here you go: the COVID-19 pandemic and the resulting sicknesses and deaths. Worldwide business shutdowns and, for many, business closures without hopes of ever reopening. Job losses. School closures. Political conflict. Racial injustice. Protests—many turned violent. Human trafficking. Widespread out-of-control wildfires. Those are just the large-scale things that come to mind for me at this moment in time.

If I take a closer, small-scale look at my own life, there are lots of things that hurt my heart right now, too: one of my best friends is suffering an unimaginable life change and long recovery with no end in sight. Friends whose children have recently been diagnosed with cancer. Friends who want to have children but are struggling with infertility. People I know are struggling with depression. Children I know with awful home life situations. People in my life who are lonely but can't have visitors due to being socially isolated because of the pandemic. It's all heartbreaking and can take over all of our thoughts.

Now, I obviously can't see into the future, and I'm hopeful that things will turn around for our world as a whole by the time anyone else reads this. But it's been pretty easy to feel frustrated, and down, and depressed, and hurt, because of all of the bad stuff happening around us.

The Scripture above reminds me of the reassuring fact that, no matter what is going on in our lives, "God's got this." The crippled man begged for help, and Peter and John gave him the kind of help that only God could give him. Jesus' disciples used their faith in Jesus and the name of Jesus to help this man walk again. When things are bad around us, may we have the kind of faithfulness in Jesus that Peter and John had. And may we always remember that, no matter what, "God's got this."

Update: As you probably noticed, some time has passed since this devotion was initially written, and you will find similar content from that time in other devotions within this book. While there were numerous things that the COVID pandemic changed in our lives, our world has moved past it in many ways. The world keeps turning, as they say. Still, in any of our lives, bad things happen. Frustrating things happen. Discouraging things happen. No matter what happens, the one thing that remains, and is the most important part of this update, is that God's *still* got this. And our God always will.

Families

One of my favorite books as a child, and now one of my own kids' favorite books, is called *Alexander and the Terrible, Horrible, No Good, Very Bad Day* by Judith Viorst. Maybe you've read it, maybe not, but either way, take a minute to find it on YouTube or in your home library to read it right now. I'll wait right here.

Welcome back! What did you think? That book describes some days I've had before: the kind of day where one thing after the next just seems to be going wrong. Have you ever had a day like that before? Sometimes, things go wrong because of the choices we make. Other times, the things that go wrong are totally out of our control. Either way, those kinds of moments and days can be very upsetting.

God knows when you're feeling upset or hurt when something goes wrong in your life. It's important to remember that God is with us, not just on our very best days but on our very worst days, too. Faithfulness means we can believe that God will guide us, strengthen us, and be with us, especially when things seem to be going wrong. On those bad days, remember that "God's got this" when it comes to everything in your life.

Prayer

Heavenly Father, help us to remember that you are with us on all of our good days and our bad days. You know all the things that are hurting our hearts. We pray that you give us the same kind of faithfulness that Jesus' disciples had. Thank you for being there to guide us, strengthen us, and be with us. We love you. Amen.

Extension Activity

Maybe you already have one, but at this time, write a prayer list together as a family. Try to include everything that may be hurting your heart right now. These things might be on a large-scale level (worldwide, national, etc.) or maybe more small-scale and personal. After writing down all the people and situations that are on your heart, say a special prayer to remember that "God's got this" in every situation in our lives.

Faithfulness

Through the big and small moments of your life, God's faithfulness shines through.

Scripture

"Being confident of this, that he who began a good work in you will carry it on to completion until the day of Christ Jesus."

– PHILIPPIANS 1:6

"Be strong and courageous. Do not be afraid; do not be discouraged, for the Lord your God will be with you wherever you go."

– JOSHUA 1:9 (EMPHASIS ADDED)

Parents

My husband and I just celebrated our fifth anniversary this past December. We got married on, quite possibly, the most frigid day of the entire year, but the magic of the day and anticipating Christmas more than made up for the snowy, freezing setting.

After we got married, Josh and I started collecting ornaments for our tree from every place that we visited together. On top of that, being married at Christmas time, many gifts that we were given were ornaments from people we love. Taking me back to Christmas traditions and memories growing up, we also inherited special ornaments and decorations from my grandparents' Christmas trees. I look at my tree, and I see a collection of the people who have impacted me the most (some of whom are now with Jesus) and places, experiences, and moments that have shaped and grown me. I look at my tree, and I see symbols and reminders of God's faithfulness over the years in ways beyond what I could have asked or imagined.

This past year of 2020 has been a year unlike any other, with every feeling and emotion under the sun! It has had confusion, joy, peace, life, chaos, hardship, slowness, stress, connection, and disconnection. In the midst of it all, sometimes, I catch myself wondering: Why? Or when will it end? Or what is the purpose of this? It is super easy to get caught up in the heaviness of it all.

This year has certainly been different, but I take encouragement reflecting today on our God, who is not. On God, who has been with us since the beginning, shining through the ornaments of people, experiences, and redemption that decorate the tree of our lives and faith. On God, who is unwavering and faithful, whose love is rooted, grounded, and steadfast, whose mercies are new each morning, whose presence is always near, whose peace is transcendent, whose hope is eternal, whose promises are secure. Even, and especially when, it doesn't make sense, I am thankful that He is steadfast, unwavering, and faithful.

Families

Have you ever played "I Spy" before or spent hours looking through *I Spy* books, trying to spot everything on the page? They're so hard—but so fun! Growing up, my dad loved to play "I Spy" with us on the Christmas tree. We would take turns picking the color of an ornament for our family members to guess. My dad, though, was pretty predictable. We had a yellow ornament of Santa wearing a yellow raincoat and rain hat, and my dad would always say, "I spy something yellow," so we always knew to keep our eyes out for that yellow Santa Claus!

Do you have favorite ornaments on your tree? Maybe the ornaments were given to you by family members or friends who love you, or maybe you picked out a really cool one from a special place that you visited! It is cool to look at those ornaments and be reminded of all of the important people, places, and events that have made you, you!

From the very beginning of your life, God has been faithful. He promises to never leave you and always be with you. He will be faithful to you forever.

Prayer

God, thank you so much for the promise of your faithfulness. When life is hard or confusing or doesn't make sense, thank you for the promise that you will always be with us and will never leave us. We are so grateful for you and the gifts of people, places, and events that remind us of your love and faithfulness. Amen.

Extension Activity

Take some time to talk about and think about your ornaments for your Christmas tree! If you're able to, take them out and look at each one, remembering its story and where it came from (Yes, even if you're reading this in July, take them out! Who says you can't celebrate Christmas year-round?!) Which ones are your favorite? Why are they special to you?

As you share stories and remember where the ornaments came from, may you be reminded of God's faithfulness in your life! He is always with you, completing the good work He has started in you each step of the way.

Faithfulness

Embrace childlike humility and wonder.

Scripture

"He called a little child to him, and placed the child among them. And he said: 'Truly I tell you, unless you change and become like little children, you will never enter the kingdom of heaven. Therefore, whoever takes the lowly position of this child is the greatest in the kingdom of heaven.'"

– MATTHEW 18:2–4

Parents

I'd like to share a conversation I had with my daughter when she was six.

Aila: Mommy, cheer for me!
Me: Why?
Aila: Because I just killed a fly.
Me: (worried it fell in her bed) Where did it go?
Aila: Heaven!

No, we don't kill bugs just for the fun of it. But I love to remember this conversation when I think about having the faith of a child. (Fun fact: The Bible doesn't phrase it as "faith like a child," but that idea comes from what Jesus says in the verse above, as well as other parts of the Gospels.) To a child, the simple idea of everyone loving Jesus and being together in Heaven someday is easy to imagine. Even a fly that flew into my daughter's bedroom for the last time.

Sometimes our faith is complicated. We ask all kinds of questions. We wonder about black and white and gray areas. We complicate things. We oversimplify or overcomplicate things. We receive conflicting messages. When there is an overload of information and thoughts bombarding our brains, of course we feel overwhelmed!

In these moments, it's important to remember what faith is. Faith is trusting in God no matter what. It is believing that His Word is Truth. While there was definitely a flaw in Aila's theology (hey, remember, she was only six), the easy faith she had was a good reminder for me then and now that our faith in God doesn't have to be complicated.

Families

When I was a teenager, I was riding in a car with my friend (who—fun fact—later became my sister's brother-in-law!). He was driving us to our destination and told me to close my eyes. I closed them and rode along for a few minutes. After a bit, I could feel his driving get a little spastic. Slightly concerned, I asked him, "What are you doing?"

"Driving," he replied. More bumps, more swerves, more unnerving driving.

Not sure what was happening, I then asked, "When can I open my eyes?"

His response? "As soon as I open mine!"

Of course, I immediately panicked and opened my eyes to see his eyes had been open the whole time (thank goodness!) and he was driving just fine, if a little intentionally twitchy to sell his "eyes closed" fib.

While I strongly recommend safe driving in all situations—I'm talking to **you,** kids... and especially, **you,** grownups!—his story reminds me of what faith means. We trust that our families will give us food and shelter and all the things we need. We trust that our friends will be there when we need them. We trust that our teachers and churches will give us good guidance. We trust that whoever is driving us will safely get us to our destination.

When we have faith in God, we can close our eyes and allow Him to drive us to where we're going. We may not know what bumps or swerves may come our way, but when we have faith in God, we trust Him with our journey in this life.

Prayer

Heavenly Father, thank you for giving us the gift of our faith in you. We are so grateful to know that, by putting our faith in you, our lives are in your hands. Help us to remember this, especially when we think we have moments we want to be the one in control. We praise you for all that you do for us and for having our lives in your hands. In your holy name we pray, Amen.

Extension Activity

It's time to go on a Faith Walk! There are many variations of the Faith Walk, but here are a few ways that could work—feel free to do more than one method or to create your own option:

Method 1: Partner up. Partner #1 puts on a blindfold, and Partner #2 navigates the blindfolded partner. It's up to you what you'll have to navigate: will you have to cross the living room? Walk around the kitchen table? Go through the backyard? Decide the course and begin! When Partner #1 reaches the final destination (or doesn't, depending on how well Partner #2 communicates!), switch places.

Method 2: One person wears a blindfold, and the remaining group members are the communicators. This is very similar to the above method, with the exception that there are multiple people giving directions to the blindfolded person.

Method 3: One person is blindfolded; one person is the guide; the remaining people are the distractors. The blindfolded person and the guide have the same roles as the partners in the first method. The big difference here is that the distractors try to make as much noise as possible in order to have the blindfolded person not be able to hear, therefore making successful navigation even more difficult.

Afterward, let's debrief: What parts of this activity were easy? What parts were more challenging? How is the blindfolded person like us as we navigate life, and how is the person(s) leading the blinded person representative of God? If you chose Method 3, what connections can you make between the distractions we may come across in our lives and the noise of the distractors in the game? What other parallels can you draw between this activity and our Faith Walk with God every day?

Faithfulness

Embrace purpose with humility;
God's grace follows.

Scripture

"Then Jesus came from Galilee to the Jordan to be baptized by John. But John tried to deter him, saying, 'I need to be baptized by you, and do you come to me?' Jesus replied, 'Let it be so now; it is proper for us to do this to fulfill all righteousness.' Then John consented. As soon as Jesus was baptized, he went up out of the water. At that moment, heaven was opened, and he saw the Spirit of God descending like a dove and alighting on him. And a voice from heaven said, 'This is my Son, whom I love; with him I am well pleased.'"

– MATTHEW 3:13-17

Parents

Some days, I am my own cheerleader, and I take this role on eagerly! Get the kids up, dressed, and on the bus in time for school? No problem, I can do it! Have a productive day at work? On it! Make dinner in time to eat before the family's activities? Yes, and with a smile! Bedtime routine with happy family members? You know it!

But some days, I feel like I can't muster up the motivation to get myself out of bed, let alone the kids. And yes, my difficult days are nowhere near as challenging as I'm sure they could be: I have a wonderful and supportive husband; I am a healthy person; I have a pair of helpful kids who generally behave; my job is enjoyable and fulfilling... I have a lot of positive things going for me. But I still have "those days" where I have to put all my effort into getting myself together. On those days, I am counting on God's faithfulness to see me through.

In the Scripture above, we read about Jesus' baptism. What always strikes me in this passage is how John seems hesitant to baptize Jesus—not because he doesn't want to, but because he believes that Jesus should be the one baptizing him. Jesus clarifies that, in order to fulfill prophecy and accomplish God's mission, John must be the one to baptize Him.

Maybe John woke up that day unsure whether he could even handle his usual tasks, let alone baptize the Son of Man! Even if he woke up fully motivated, I can only imagine the number of questions and concerns running through his mind when Jesus asked him to do something so significant.

Still, Jesus reminded John of his vital role in "fulfilling all righteousness," and John consented—because of his faith in Jesus. What an affirmation it must have been when God sent a dove and a voice from heaven to express approval of His Son and His actions!

On the days when I'm slowly embracing the gift of the day, I want to remember this passage. Jesus pursued John the Baptist, whose faithfulness allowed him to put Jesus first, in order for Jesus' mission to mankind to continue to be fulfilled through his baptism. I want to remember that, likewise, Jesus is pursuing us to continue to do his will so that we can bring God's light to further His kingdom here on Earth. Because John the Baptist had faith and baptized Jesus, Jesus was able to go on to do all the important things in his life, including giving us the most important gift of all—the promise of salvation through his death on the cross.

Families

Sometimes my kids tell me that they feel lonely. They might feel lonely at home when they're not getting my full attention. They might feel left out at school because of friendship difficulties with their classmates. They might feel excluded on their teams because they don't have a close buddy with them.

I always feel sad to hear this. I'm glad they can tell me, and we try to work through it together. I want to remind you, too, that you can always find a grown-up in your life to talk to whenever you're feeling alone.

My own parents told me when I was a young child that if I have Jesus in my heart, I am never truly alone. I can talk to Him all the time and tell Him what I'm going through. I still remember that important lesson, even as a thirty-eight-year-old parent myself!

In the Bible passage above, we read about John the Baptist, who baptized Jesus. John didn't think it was right for him to baptize Jesus. In fact, he asked, *"Shouldn't* ***you*** *be baptizing* ***me*** *instead?"* But Jesus told John that He needed him.

Likewise, Jesus wants us to have faith that He will use us to accomplish His will in our lives. He was able to use John the Baptist in important ways. I pray that you, too, will allow Jesus to use you in meaningful ways in your life.

Prayer

Heavenly Father, thank you for the reminder that John the Baptist was pursued by Jesus. Help us to remember that we are also being pursued to do God's will in our lives each and every day and to be with you, especially in the times when we have a hard time even getting out of bed, or in the times when we are lonely. Help us to have faith that you will use us in important ways in our lives. In your holy name we pray, Amen.

Extension Activity

Intentionality Links: Today, use this passage to set intentional reminders of God's presence in your life. Cut strips of paper. (You might want to start with seven and do one each day this week. You can always add more to see how long it can go!) Each day, take notice of a way that God is using you to share his good news with others. Did you help a friend who was feeling lonely? Write it on your strip and loop it together. The next day, do the same thing! Did you share kindness with a stranger by smiling at them and saying hello? Write it on your next strip of paper, loop it around the first, and connect it into a ring.

At the end of your week, look to see all the ways God was using you in your life. Have faith that you might not even see all the ways God is using you, but rejoice in all the ways you *can* see Him using you to share His love with others!

Faithfulness

Trust fully in God; He provides and fulfills your heart's desires.

Scripture

"Trust in the Lord, and do good; dwell in the land and befriend faithfulness. Delight yourself in the Lord, and he will give you the desires of your heart. Commit your way to the Lord; trust in him, and he will act."

– PSALM 37:3-5

Parents

Today, on our drive home from church, we saw a terrible accident. It was a scary scene to witness: a big pickup truck was turned on its side; two other vehicles were beat up. A major intersection was blocked off, and many emergency personnel were taking photos, helping move the debris, and directing traffic around the accident.

My husband, Andy, and I intently discussed what we saw: how did that pickup flip to its side like that, and at that particular spot in the road? What part did the other vehicles play in the accident? We put our scientist hats on and tried to figure out the logistics of the accident. Meanwhile, our kids were quiet observers in the backseat until our youngest, Archie, spoke up: "Mommy, will you pray for the people in the accident?"

I felt my heart change and honored my son's request. We said a prayer for the people involved in the accident, for those who were helping at the scene, and for peace and care for everyone else witnessing the accident. (Archie piped up at the end of the prayer to add, "Be with anyone else in the world who is hurting." More points for that kiddo!)

Sometimes we get caught up in how things work, or we focus on figuring out the meaning of the things we see or experience. How often, though, should we turn to prayer instead of trying to figure everything else out? When we allow God to speak to us through the prayer that we offer Him, we can be in constant communication with Him as He helps us to figure out what's truly important. May we be reminded by this little message—brought to you by the childlike faith of the young ones in our lives—to remember to pray in every circumstance.

Families

Have you ever seen anything scary happen? Maybe you saw someone get hurt, or a car accident, or maybe you even had to face a fear of yours (like spiders or snakes... or is that just me?).

Sometimes when we focus on our fears, they can take over our lives! It can be all we think about, and we can be in a constant state of worry over our fear.

My family saw an upsetting car accident on our way home from church today. It was scary to look at, and I started to let the fear take over. That's when I heard a sweet voice from the backseat: my son, Archie, asked us if we could pray for the people who were in the accident. We closed our eyes (except for my husband, who was driving, of course!) and said a prayer for the people in the accident and the helpers at the scene of the accident.

When we said "Amen," my heart was calm, and I could feel God in my heart. I knew, no matter what happened in the scary accident, that God was with not only us but also the people involved in the crash.

I am thankful for Archie reminding me to pray when I felt sad and afraid. God is always ready to listen to us, especially in those moments that are out of our control—because they are always in His control.

Prayer

Lord God, we are so thankful that you are always ready to listen to our prayers. Thank you for being with us in those moments, when we feel sad, afraid, and like things are out of our control. Please help us to remember to call on you, no matter what is going on in our lives. In your name we pray, Amen.

Extension Activity

Start a prayer journal. It can be a family prayer journal, where you share things that you can all pray for together. You can also each do your own personal prayer journals, if that works better for your family. And hey! What is that kindness journal from earlier in this devotional doing these days? Is it time to dust it off and repurpose it as a prayer journal? Or have you been using it all this time? Either way, go you! You are an amazing journaling family, and I'm so proud of you for taking the time to reflect on some pretty important things through your journaling.

So back to your prayer journal: Write down the date and the things and people you want to pray for. There are many ways to keep a prayer journal: you can write down the person's name or the concern you have, or you can even write out the whole prayer.

In any moments of fear and worry, be sure to add those concerns to your prayer journal. Each time you add a prayer topic or concern to your journal, look back and reflect on the prayers you've added previously. As you read through them, pay close attention to any ways that you see God answering your prayers.

Faithfulness

Be filled with the hope
that only God can provide.

Scripture

"Be strong and courageous. Do not be afraid or terrified because of them, for the Lord your God goes with you; he will never leave you nor forsake you."

– DEUTERONOMY 31:6

Parents

Do you ever pay attention to the predictive text on your phone? (If you aren't following me, I'm talking about the suggested words that your phone offers as you type a message.) Sometimes the suggestions on mine crack me up. Apparently, I have used *"Thanksgiving"* enough for that to be one of the most frequent suggestions after I type *"happy."* I guess, at one point, I sent a lot of *"Happy Thanksgiving"* text messages to my family and friends. I must have been super pumped for turkey season!

Another of my most frequent words that comes up in my predictive texts is the word "hopefully." (Now, this one I can understand a bit better than the Thanksgiving one.) When I reply to texts from friends, I can just see my practically automatic hopeful response. If a friend texts something like, "My son has another ear infection," I'm sure I'd say, "Oh no! Poor guy... *hopefully* he feels better soon." Or if my husband gives me an update on his lengthy dissertation writing process for his doctoral program, I would probably say, "I'm so proud of you! *Hopefully,* you hear good news back from the professor this week!" Or maybe my friend invites me to go to a show with her; I'd say something like, "Ooh, yes, please! We have a busy weekend, but *hopefully* I can rearrange a few things to make it!"

Hope is one thing we can offer people in almost any circumstance. The verse above reminds us that we can be strong and courageous, to *hope* for things, and that God goes with us wherever we go. Our faithfulness and hope in Him can be something we lean on daily and can be an encouragement to those in our lives.

Families

What are some things that you hope for in your life? Maybe you hope to get to spend some quality time with a special person in your life. You might hope to hear good news from your teacher about a test you took. Hey, I wonder if you hope to eat your favorite meal for dinner tonight! Maybe your hopes are dreams of what you might get to do or be someday: A teacher? A dancer? An author? All those things?

I tend to be a very hopeful person, but living life with a hope-filled mindset can be challenging at times. In those moments when I need a bit more hopefulness, I remember that God is right in the middle of all of everything I'm going through: God is the one who is beside me all the time. When I have hope in the things God has planned for my life, I am able to be positive and optimistic about my circumstances, no matter what they may be.

If we are feeling like we need a bit of hope in our lives, we can ask God to provide it for us. The verse above reminds us that God is with us, no matter what. That can give us hope in our best moments and also those not-so-good moments. We can have faith and hope in Him and remember that our strong, courageous faith in Him means He will always be with us.

Prayer

Heavenly Father, we pray that you fill us with hope! Regardless of the circumstances we may find ourselves in, we are so thankful to find hope in the plan you have for our lives. Thank you for the promise to never leave us or forsake us. May our hopes and dreams be a reflection of your will for our lives, and give us faith to know that you are with us always. In your name we pray, Amen.

Extension Activity

One of my favorite books to read with my elementary students is *The Miraculous Journey of Edward Tulane* by Kate DiCamillo. A particular quote I love to read each time we arrive at that part of the story is: "You must be filled with expectancy. You must be awash in hope."

Over the next week or two, read aloud this book together as a family. (I'm sure the local library has a copy! Raise your hand if you're a huge library fan, like I am!) Talk about the ways Edward changes his attitude about hope throughout the story. (Warning: I cry multiple times every time I read it. There is some sensitive content, but it's a beautiful story worth reading when you're ready for it.) Discuss ways that Edward's life changes as he allows himself to be hopeful.

Gentleness

The fruit we chose to represent *Gentleness* is the *Banana*. The inside of a banana can be easily bruised or squished, even with the peel on it. This is a fitting reminder that we must have gentleness so as not to cause any damage with our words or actions toward others.

Gentleness

Choose gentle words; they bring peace and calm to conflicts.

Scripture

"A gentle answer turns away wrath, but a harsh word stirs up anger."

– PROVERBS 15:1

Parents

Say it with me: Gentleness. Even the word itself is calming, sweet, and soothing. I think our culture has a tendency to see gentleness as weakness, but I strongly disagree with that. When I think of someone showing gentleness, I see someone who cares enough about who or what they are addressing to treat it with tender care.

How much easier is it to be harsh and careless than it is to be gentle? This particular Fruit of the Spirit is a hard pill for me to swallow when I feel like being harsh and critical to those around me. If I'm being honest, a lot of the time, my harshness is me taking my bad day or frustrations out on those around me.

Really, though, the reminder to care for others by showing them gentleness is so important in our daily lives. The verse above from Proverbs is a huge reminder to me as a parent, but also in my other relationships and human interactions. How many people do I come across and am quick to respond harshly to? The people who take my turn at the four-way stop sign right by my work. The people (my own little ones, especially) who need my help when it's inconvenient for me. The people who take too long in front of me at the drive-through. The people who think rules don't apply to them and do whatever they want without thinking of how it impacts others, including me. The people who leave a mess for me to clean up in my house. (Again, looking at you, sweet offspring of mine!)

Conversely, how many people do I interact with throughout my day who I have the opportunity to show gentleness to? How much gentler are my actions if, instead, at that four-way stop sign, I let someone go ahead of me even if it was—gasp!—my turn?! What did that truly take for me to show a simple, gentle gesture?

This pause to offer gentleness also gives us a moment to think about why someone might be acting in their own harsh way. How do I know why that person wanted to get through the four-way intersection so quickly? Were they late for work? Were they distracted by the kids in the backseat and didn't realize it wasn't their turn? Are they at a time of struggle or stress in general in their life, and traffic just adds to it? I have no idea what it's like to be in their shoes. And often I am caught up in my own life and disregard what they may be going through. It's in these times that we need to remember to choose the gentle act, instead of the harsh one, whenever the opportunity allows.

Families

What does it mean to be gentle? Share with someone who is reading this with you what the word "gentle" means to you. Go ahead; we'll be right here when you're done.

What did you share? Did you say that the word "gentle" means kind or mild? Did you say it means "peaceful" or "tender"? Gentleness can mean all of these things. Maybe you had another idea about gentleness. Great job!

The Bible tells us to use gentle words instead of harsh words (see the verse from Proverbs above). Sometimes it's really hard to be gentle. Think of a time when, instead of being gentle, you were harsh. Why did you act in a harsh way? Think about that same time. Could you have been gentle instead? How?

All of us have had moments when we forget to be gentle, even grownups! (Sometimes especially grownups!) This devotion about gentleness is a reminder to take a minute when you are on the verge of having a harsh reaction to something around you. Maybe you want to call a name to someone who was mean to you. Maybe you want to yell at someone who is telling you to do something you don't want to do. Maybe you're just feeling tired or cranky—again, the grownups reading this with you have been tired and cranky before, too!

Now take a minute to think about a time when you showed gentleness. Maybe you helped a younger kid who was feeling sad. Maybe you said a kind word to your parent when they were in a bad mood. Maybe you sent a gentle, encouraging card to a friend who was on your mind. Why did you choose to be gentle in that instance? The next time you feel yourself deciding between a harsh or a gentle response, remember this Proverb that reminds us of the importance of being gentle. Instead of responding in a harsh way, try to share gentleness with others whenever you can.

Prayer

Lord God, we are so grateful that you have given us the option to choose gentleness in our words and actions toward others. Please help us remember to be gentle toward others, especially when we feel like we want to react harshly to them. Please forgive us for the times when we have forgotten to be gentle toward others, and we ask that you create in us a gentle heart. Amen.

Extension Activity

For this Fruit of the Spirit activity about gentleness, you're going to need two actual pieces of the same type of fruit. ● Apples or pears would work well. (Fair warning: You won't want to eat at least one of these when you're done!) First, start by being gentle with the first piece of fruit. Pass it along in a circle with your family. Roll it carefully back and forth. Gently toss it to someone nearby who will cradle it when they catch it.

Now, get ready to be harsh! With adult permission, find creative ways to treat that second poor piece of fruit harshly. Throw the apple or pear as far as you can into the yard. Smash it on your driveway floor. Toss it as high into the air as you can and let it fall to the ground. Do you have a baseball bat or a golf club? Again, **with parent permission,** feel free to take out your harshness on the piece of fruit.

Once you're done, gather what's left of both pieces of fruit. Compare them. Clearly, one of them has endured a lot of harsh treatment, while the other was treated much more gently.

Talk about how this demonstration relates to our Scripture for today. After enduring the gentle and harsh actions, which fruit was in good shape? Which fruit wasn't? How do our own gentle words and actions relate to how the pieces of fruit ended up? How do our own harsh words and actions relate to how the pieces of fruit ended up?

The next time you need to remember to choose a gentle word or action, remember this activity. Remember how your gentleness and harshness impacted the piece of fruit, and how your own words and actions can have the same impact on others around you.

Gentleness

Embrace humility, gentleness, and patience, supporting each other with compassion and love.

Scripture

"Be completely humble and gentle; be patient, bearing with one another in love."

– EPHESIANS 4:2

Parents

"Be gentle!" I feel like I have said these words 857 times over the past few months, as Jack learns how to interact with our five-year-old, rambunctious, full-sized Goldendoodle, Copper. Since he has been old enough, his first instinct has been to take fistfuls of his curly, red hair and squeeze and pull it as hard as he can with a giant smile on his face. Thankfully, Copper has tolerated his exuberant greeting. To say the least, Copper is Jack's best friend, but Jack isn't always Copper's! We have had to practice how to be gentle **a lot** with Jack, and although we're starting to do a little more petting than pulling, it always eventually gets taken a little too far.

Similarly to Jack, I think when we interact with others, it is easy sometimes to just want to pull as hard as we can, rather than going in lightly, especially when we feel we have been wronged. When we're mad, frustrated, stressed, or angry, it's natural to enter interactions and situations with our guards up and tongues ready to fire off a remark, rather than go in with humility and gentleness.

I love this Scripture from Ephesians because it prompts us to surrender our feelings to the Lord... not just partially, but God calls us to *completely* be humble and gentle. When I picture that, I picture the emptying of all negative thoughts and feelings and God pouring in His humility and gentleness, wholly filled with His gentleness, love, and grace. I think that when we come with a spirit of gentleness, God can open our eyes to the truth of the situation, rather than our perception being tainted by our own thoughts and feelings. He can allow us to see others and situations in their purest form, rather than our morphed, befuddled ones.

I have found that in many moments, gentleness doesn't always come easily. When you've tried to explain directions multiple times and they aren't being followed or you feel like you're not being heard, it is easy to view others by their mistakes and shortcomings rather than their hearts and souls. It is easy to want to respond with "Why do you always act like this?" rather than approaching the situation with gentleness and patience. This verse is grounding and recentering, as it helps us to respond from a place of calm rather than anger, to view others as children of God and extend grace, rather than defining them by how they've frustrated us or let us down. Empty yourself and let God fill you with all humility and gentleness today.

Families

Growing up, I loved to watch TV Land and tune in to the classic show *The Brady Bunch*. If you have never seen it, it stars the Bradys, who have three daughters and three sons, a mom and a dad, and a beloved housekeeper named Alice. Their house is filled to the brim!

In one of the episodes, the Brady kids are playing football in the house, even though they were told not to. When a throw goes wrong, the ball crashes into a fragile vase, causing it to break and shatter everywhere. Their lack of care and gentleness led to the vase being destroyed.

Have your parents ever reminded you to be gentle around breakable things? If you're holding a special glass or fragile item, it is important to hold it very carefully and gently.

Just like we need to treat breakable items carefully, God also wants us to treat others with the same gentleness. We wouldn't take a glass and handle it roughly or throw it on the table. Instead, we would hold it with lots of focus and care. In the same way, God wants us to be gentle with our words and actions towards others so we don't cause any damage to their hearts. He wants us to be patient and gentle when we talk with others so that we can respect them and really listen to them.

How can you be more gentle today?

Prayer

Dear God, we confess that sometimes we enter situations a little too roughly. Help us to be more gentle with our words and actions, even when we feel frustrated or angry. Please empty us of any feelings that keep us from loving others, and fill us with your gentleness and patience. Amen.

Extension Activity

Rather than recreating the *Brady Bunch* scene and throwing a football in the house, we're going to practice gentleness with the ultimate game: water balloon toss. Head outside, fill some water balloons, and grab a partner! Stand a few steps away from each other and toss the water balloon back and forth. Each time you complete a pass, take a step back! See how many times you can pass it back and forth (and how far apart you end up from each other). Be gentle when handling the water balloon, or else you or your partner will end up pretty wet!

Gentleness

Clothe yourself in kindness, patience, and love. Forgive freely, speak wisely, and let love unify and protect your path.

Scripture

"Therefore, as God's chosen people, holy and dearly loved, clothe yourselves with compassion, kindness, humility, gentleness, and patience. Bear with each other and forgive one another if any of you has a grievance against someone. Forgive as the Lord forgave you. And over all these virtues put on love, which binds them all together in perfect unity."

– COLOSSIANS 3:12-14

"Those who guard their mouths and their tongues keep themselves from calamity."

– PROVERBS 21:23

Parents

Have you ever found yourself trying to backtrack after misspeaking? I have, unfortunately, experienced this more than I'd like to admit. It's the worst feeling to regret my words and to know I have spoken out of turn when I could have instead spoken out of love and gentleness.

As I may have already mentioned, I am involved in local theater. While many positive, uplifting things have come from my involvement in dramatic productions, I am going to share a story about a time that was, well, less than positive.

Years ago, during a show I was performing in, we gathered backstage during intermission. Another actor asked a general question about her performance and wondered if it had been "off" at all. I hardly gave it any thought before answering that, yes, her usually spotless performance may have been slightly off that evening.

Wait, what? What in the world was I thinking?! Oh, the calamity! (to use an excellent word choice from the above proverb—though I found myself in a not excellent circumstance after opening my big mouth...)

I had no right to say what I had said. I was only speaking to what I was able to hear over the antiquated sound system that piped the onstage sound into the backstage area. I wasn't in the audience to make a judgment call on *anyone's* performance (not that even *that* would have been okay!). Not to mention, my words were not supportive, kind, gentle, or any of those important things we should try to be as Christians.

After securely putting my foot in my mouth, I immediately tried to backtrack: I just kept talking to try to get myself out of it. I asked if her performance was off, maybe because of the sound system feedback we kept hearing? Was she tired? Was it hard to focus due to the crowd dynamics? The more I talked, the deeper I dug a hole I couldn't escape. Eventually, the conversation went in another direction, and I missed an opportunity to apologize just then. Thoroughly embarrassed by my thoughtless choice, I never sought her out to try to make things right, and I continue to feel bad about it all these years later.

If I had only held my tongue or spoken in a gentle way, I wouldn't have caused any hurt feelings with my careless words. (And unfortunately, this is just one of many examples where my careless or sharp tongue has gotten me into trouble. The Lord knows I have been working on it my whole life!)

The Scripture above gives me such a wonderful mental picture when I read it. And while I feel terrible about those moments I have spoken out of impulse (and *not* gentleness), what an inspiring concept to "clothe" ourselves with so many beautiful qualities! (And, if we keep reading, we also should recognize the much-needed reminder of God's forgiveness. I definitely need that as I reflect on my mistakes.) It's not always easy to present myself in a way that embodies all of these important but often difficult qualities. May this passage remind me—and anyone else who finds themselves in similar situations—to speak gently. That way, we can be reflective of God's love through what we say and how we say it.

Families

Have you ever said something to someone that you knew hurt their feelings? Unfortunately, I have, too, probably more times than I even know.

What happens when we say something we shouldn't have said? Sometimes we keep talking or defending ourselves. Maybe we talk back, justifying what we said, to try to dig ourselves out of the hole we've dug. But when we do that, what is really happening? We are probably just digging a bigger hole. The words we say can create quite a mess for us. (Yes, sadly, I know this firsthand.)

What should we do to avoid saying something unkind? There are two things that can work almost every time. (Both of them follow pretty smart advice from some old sayings that go along with the Bible verses above.)

1. "If you don't have anything nice to say, don't say anything at all." In other words, try to think about what you say before you say it. If you are considering saying something unkind, think again and hold your tongue before you say it.

2. "You catch more flies with honey than with vinegar." What does this mean? While there may be several interpretations, my personal interpretation simply encourages us to speak in a kind, gentle way to people. They will be more receptive to what we have to say if we say something kindly and gently.

To sum it up, sometimes we might be tempted to say something thoughtless or mean. In these situations, sometimes it's good not to say anything at all, and sometimes it's good to say it with gentleness. Ask God to help you know what to say and how to say it.

Prayer

Lord, we pray that you will guide us when we speak. Help us to say things in a gentle way so that what we are saying can be heard with accepting ears. Please help us to remember that the way we speak and what we say can be a representation of Your Son living in us, and guide us to say things in a way that brings glory to you. In your holy name we pray, Amen.

Extension Activity

You will need a full tube of toothpaste for this activity. (I recommend getting a very inexpensive brand, because you won't be needing it for any dental reasons!) All set? Let's go.

1. First, squeeze all the toothpaste out of the tube. I recommend squeezing it onto a paper plate (hang onto the toothpaste you've emptied, because we will use it later). Really work hard to get every last bit of toothpaste out of that bottle. Go ahead and squeeeeeeeeeeeze, as long as it takes!
2. Now pause. Please don't read ahead until you've done the toothpaste squeeze part of the activity. Thanks for following my very specific rules.
3. Are you ready for the next part? Okay, now go ahead and put all the toothpaste back into the tube. Yep, all of it. Put it all back into the tube.

Take as long as you need. Go ahead; I'll be here when you're done. About finished then? How did that go? Were you able to get every single bit of toothpaste back into the tube?

Nope, I gave you a pretty impossible task. But one with a very important message: when you say something, it's been said and can't be taken back. Like the toothpaste, words can't be undone or unsaid once they leave your mouth. Yes, you might be able to apologize for what you have said or try to talk your way out of what you said, but the words will always remain spoken. It's important that the words we say are said in a kind and gentle way, because there is no going back once they come out of our mouths. As a little reminder, every time you squeeze toothpaste onto your toothbrush, ask God to remind you to speak in a gentle way.

Gentleness

Seek righteousness, faith, love,
endurance, and gentleness.

Scripture

"But you, man of God, flee from all this, and pursue righteousness, godliness, faith, love, endurance, and gentleness."

– 1 TIMOTHY 6:11

Parents

During the summer in between my junior and senior years at college, I traveled to Argentina to complete the study abroad requirement for my Spanish degree. The story I am about to share with you could be a book itself (and who knows, maybe it will be someday!), but I will do my best to sum it up briefly for this devotion.

The family I stayed with had a separate apartment building on their property that was just for me. It had a bedroom, a small kitchen, a bathroom, and an extra room. To heat the whole unit, there was one gas heater I had to light with matches. (Yes, it was winter there when I went. I guess that's what I get for going to the opposite hemisphere during summer break!)

One night, the heater in the room malfunctioned, releasing carbon monoxide. I was exposed to it for ten to twelve hours. To make a very long story short, miracle after miracle happened to result in my full recovery. However, I was in a coma for nine days. During that time, my parents were told to come to Argentina (to essentially claim my body, as I was not expected to survive, and if I did, the doctors said I would be in a permanent vegetative state).

While I was in the coma, I remember hearing activity from the hospital and voices of those around me. As I gradually came out of the coma, I was able to fully understand what people were saying, though I was still intubated and couldn't communicate.

One thing I remember hearing, clear as day, during this time is my mom talking to me about the accident. Now, my mom is probably one of the kindest people in the whole world, and she was a preschool teacher for many years prior to this accident. So when she was explaining to me exactly what happened, she was talking to me like I was one of the preschool students she taught. She was repeatedly telling me things, in her talking-to-a-young-child voice, like, "Amy, you were in an accident, but you're going to be okay. You're in Argentina, and you were in an accident, but you are with me and your dad."

Of course, I was still coming out of a coma (and still intubated at that point), so I couldn't politely ask her to talk to me like I was her adult child. But there was something about the gentleness with which she was telling me what was going on. Of course, I was still very confused as I eventually came out of the coma and only had the minor detail that I was in an accident. (What kind? Was everyone else in my host family safe? What exactly caused it?) But in the moment, despite my giving her a hard time about "talking to me like I was a preschooler," I was so thankful for my mom's gentleness as I returned to a fully conscious state. We all can appreciate a gentle spirit when we are on the receiving end.

Families

Sometimes sad things happen in our lives, and it can be hard to navigate the feelings that we may have when something sad happens to us. If something bad or sad happens to us or someone we love, it's okay to feel angry, upset, frustrated, or devastated. Adults and kids alike might have very big feelings when something upsetting happens.

Recently, my two nephews' uncle passed away. It was a very devastating situation; he had been sick for a long time and was still very young when he died.

My eight-year-old nephew was with me at church camp the week before his uncle passed. During chapel time, we allowed the campers to share what was on their hearts. He stood up front and shared with all of the campers and counselors what was going on. "My uncle is going to pass away," he said. "So I wanted to say a prayer." He then proceeded to pray for the situation and asked God to be with him and all of them during the situation. It was very touching, and his heartfelt prayer brought tears to my eyes.

When my sister came to pick him up, I asked her how she and her husband were feeling about everything. I also asked about her younger boy. She told me that he said, "The doctors can't heal him, but Jesus can."

My young nephew's response to the sad situation was a touching display of gentleness amid something very upsetting. His demonstration of love and a gentle spirit was a beautiful example of gentleness in a difficult time.

Prayer

Heavenly Father, we ask that you be with us in difficult times. When we lose a loved one or something sad happens to us or those we know, help us to work through any emotions we may feel. Help us to always remember to lean on you and your wisdom during challenging times, and that you may give us a spirit of love and gentleness as we know you are with us. In your holy name we pray, Amen.

Extension Activity

Sometimes, when things make us sad, we may not know how to work through our feelings. Today, I will share two things you can do to help when someone goes through something sad. Maybe it's losing a pet or a loved one, or moving to a new place and feeling the loss of your old home, or maybe it's a difficult situation that you have had to endure.

The first thing you can do is to create a memory box. Get a box of some type—a shoebox, an old lunchbox, or any container. Feel free to decorate the box to make it extra special. Then, inside, put things that remind you of the person or thing you may have lost. You could write a letter, print a photo, draw a picture, put in a particular item, or whatever you decide should be included, and put it in the memory box. You can look in the box anytime you think about the person or thing you lost.

The second thing you can do is to create a memory book. You can use a notebook, journal, or binder. On the pages of your memory book, you can put the same items as you would in the memory box: write stories or letters, add photos or hand-drawn pictures, anything that you decide should be included. Again, look through the memory book whenever that person or thing comes to mind.

I just want to add: If you haven't experienced the pain of great loss and these activities don't seem to be relevant to you right now, you may choose to use something special to you and create a memory box or a memory book for that thing or person instead.

Gentleness

We are saved by grace, a gift from God, given freely through faith.

Scripture

"He has saved us and called us to a holy life—not because of anything we have done but because of his own purpose and grace. This grace was given us in Christ Jesus before the beginning of time."

– 2 TIMOTHY 1:9

"For it is by grace you have been saved through faith, and this is not from yourselves; it is the gift of God, not by works, so that no one can boast."

– EPHESIANS 2:8–9

"This righteousness is given through faith in Jesus Christ to all who believe. There is no difference between Jew and Gentile, for all have sinned and fall short of the glory of God, and all are justified freely by his grace through the redemption that came by Christ Jesus."

– ROMANS 3:22–24

Parents

Although I am not a "One" on the Enneagram, I struggle with perfectionism. I am my own worst critic. I'm one of those people who, if I feel I hurt someone or messed up, I will replay the situation in my head a thousand times, figuring out where I went wrong or beating myself up for the way I worded something! I am extremely hard on myself and struggle to give myself grace. (If you're unfamiliar with the Enneagram numbers and their meanings, I encourage you to look them up! It's very interesting to find out about yourself.)

When my husband and I felt ready to start a family, it took a while before Jack came along. In my head, I thought that as soon as we were ready, it would happen! So when a year passed by and nothing was happening, I was discouraged and questioned what was wrong with me. I was really stressed with work and was bringing a lot of my stress home. That, in turn, was affecting my health in many ways, which made me even harder on myself! I was stressed about being stressed, which made me more stressed! Why couldn't I be less tense? What was wrong with me? Why couldn't I calm down and make this one thing happen that we hoped for so badly?

I remember sharing this with a friend, and she calmly and wisely responded, "You can never thwart the plans God has for you." Wow. It hit me so hard. I immediately started crying and felt all this pent-up stress and anger I had been holding and putting on myself slowly release. God spoke through her to me that day, and it was like a wave of peace washed over me. I heard God say, *"Be gentle with yourself."* This wasn't my fault. I was doing the best I could and needed to give myself grace. His plan and timing would be perfect, and I needed to rest in that.

My grandpa was a Presbyterian minister, and his whole life was devoted to sharing the gospel. Even when he was 100 years old, he was still preaching and witnessing to others in the nursing home where he and my grandmother lived. We used to do a small service every month for the people on the third floor of the building, with the most skilled care, and he often gave the message. Almost every service he shared Romans 3, and I can still hear him saying, "We all fall short of the glory of God."

He knew at his age that although he lived an amazing life in service to Christ, nothing he did or didn't do would earn him any eternal value. Every breath was a gift from God, and His destiny was thanks to Christ alone and His gift on the cross to us.

It is easy to put unnecessary pressure on, or be hard on ourselves. But my prayer for myself and for you is that we can give ourselves grace and treat ourselves gently. We are human and live in a broken world. Life is just plain hard sometimes! But we are held and guided by a God who loves us through it all and treats us gently as we fall, learn, and try again. May we learn to treat ourselves with that same love and grace.

Families

I have always been really hard on myself. I remember being in an English class in sixth grade, and we had been assigned a seventeen-point grammar worksheet for homework. I didn't realize that it was going to be graded, and although I tried my best on it, I didn't really spend a lot of time on it and turned it in after completing it without much care or thought.

The next day, we got our papers back, and, to my dismay, in a giant red marker, was a big letter "F." Not only had I missed spotting a bunch of grammatical errors in the letter, but I also had majorly failed the worksheet. I had never failed an assignment in my life! What were my parents going to say?

Keep in mind, this was a grammar *worksheet*. Not a quiz, not a test, not a final, but a worksheet. However, you would have thought that I had just experienced a major loss by my reaction, as I immediately burst into uncontrollable tears (actually more so, **sobs**). My teacher tried to encourage me, saying it truly wasn't a big deal, but seeing that bold, bright

"F" was seared into my mind. My face turned blotchy and red, and I had to go to the bathroom to try to calm down. I remember feeling like I was a total and complete failure!

That day, I was absolutely ashamed when I got home from school. I distinctly remember going into my room and lying down on my bed. My mom came in and asked what was wrong, and I couldn't even bring myself to tell her. In my eyes, my parents were perfect! I had majorly let them down. Thankfully, she already knew, as my teacher had called home, worried about me.

That night my mom and dad both talked with me, and I remember them sharing stories about how they had failed and messed up growing up. It was the first time I realized that my parents aren't perfect after all. They assured me that it's okay if I mess up and that I can always learn from it, and that a mistake doesn't define me or change who I am.

The cool thing is that God doesn't define you by your mistakes either! You don't earn your way to heaven by what you do or do not do. Rather, it is a gift from God! God's grace for you never runs out, and just as God is gentle with you, you too should be gentle with yourself.

Prayer

Dear God, thank you for the gift of Your Son and the knowledge that nothing can separate us from your love. Just as you so lovingly give us grace, help us to be gentle with ourselves as we learn and grow, knowing that as we make mistakes, we are held and loved by you. In Jesus' name, Amen.

Extension Activity

One of my favorite games to play at indoor recess was *Jenga!* My friends and I would sit around the stacked tower of blocks and carefully pull each block until the tower collapsed. It is a game that requires patience, but most of all, gentleness!

Your challenge this week is to find a *Jenga* game (or create your own with blocks at home!) and practice pulling each block with your best gentleness! While you play, think about how you can be gentle with yourself this week (or with others!)

Self-Control

The final fruit we chose is the *Apple* for *Self-Control.* We have chosen to use a green apple, which can be very sour and a challenge to swallow (like so many things in our lives that require self-control). Green can also represent envy, like the envy we may have toward people who demonstrate the self-control we desire. Lastly, many people also associate the apple with the forbidden fruit that Adam and Eve ate in the Garden of Eden, so there are plenty of Self-Control connections we can make with their story in the Bible.

Self-Control

is Crazy Cool

Self-Control

Live with strength,
love, and courage.

Scripture

"For the Spirit God gave us does not make us timid, but gives us power, love and self-discipline."

– 2 TIMOTHY 1:7

Parents

We recently celebrated the New Year and all of the promises that come with the turning of a page, or a new chapter, or a whole new book—however you look at it. I've always loved the idea of a clean slate, the way a fresh new year comes in with its hopes and dreams, new goals and resolutions. (This particular New Year was 2021, so it didn't have much work to do in terms of improvement... Its predecessor, 2020, was such a mess in so many ways for so many people. So, as a meme I read said something along the lines of, *"There's no way you can mess up as badly as 2020 did. You don't have to do* ***anything****, 2021."* That was very true.)

Like many others, I usually pick a typical New Year's resolution: eat better, exercise more, lose that pesky weight (especially since it had been creeping up during the COVID-19 quarantine). As much as I knew that reaching those goals would be nice, I know myself. I know that, as motivated as I might be to make those changes initially, it went deeper than superficial self-improvement. I needed help with the self-control area of my life.

In a time of reflection, I thought about how God reminds us to have a spirit of power, love, and self-control, as the verse above says. I thought about what that meant specifically in my life. How could I focus my time and energy on God? And by focusing on Him, He could give me the self-control I needed to make improvements that were not, in fact, superficial, but in actuality, healthy decisions: decisions that could help me be more present, more energized, more focused, more able to share His love with others because I, myself, wasn't so depleted.

After some consideration, I realized that as a "list" person, I need a specific plan, and one that I could stick to. My plan included a daily checklist with tiny daily goals. But my plan didn't focus on weight loss and working out. Instead, I made a goal to spend more time reading God's Word daily. I made a goal to spend more time on my daily devotions. And I made another goal to spend time journaling about, reflecting on, and writing down what God was teaching me through my time spent with Him. (Full disclosure: I also made goals to walk more and take care of what I was putting into my body. But that wasn't the main focus of my plan.)

I'll be honest, at the time I'm writing this, I'm still pretty early in the process of my self-control New Year's resolutions. But if I've learned anything in this life, it's that our life is about the journey. It's about the process. It's about growing, learning, and being open to what God has offered us. And when we allow God to guide us through self-controlled decisions and actions, there are more things for us to do to glorify His kingdom than we'd ever imagined.

Families

Take a minute to reread today's Scripture. What are the things God has given us? That's right: a spirit of power, love, and self-control. We're taking a close look at that last one, self-control.

Self-control is one of those tricky concepts. I'll let you in on a secret: sometimes, kids might think having self-control is something only *they* find difficult. But guess what: adults also sometimes struggle to have self-control, too. In fact, sometimes adults lack self-control wayyyyy more than kids do! While most adults don't stomp around when we don't get our way, or throw a fit when something upsets us, or yell and scream to express our feelings, we sometimes lack self-control in very different ways. Whether you're 4, 14, or 104, self-control is something that God reminds us to have.

Can you name some situations in your life when you tend to lose your self-control? Is it when a friend upsets you, and you respond meanly toward them? Is it when a parent tells you to do something you don't want to do, so you throw a fit? Is it when you know you should be praying as much as possible, but you would rather do something else and impulsively do that instead? Identify ways you might need help with self-control. Then, write them down and pray about them. Ask God to help you have self-control in the times when you struggle with it. Pray for His strength to help you have self-control, especially in the moments when you really need His help.

Prayer

Heavenly Father, thank you for giving us a spirit of power, love, and self-control. Please help us remember to exercise self-control in our lives, especially in those moments when it is difficult for us. Give us the discernment to follow you and your will for our lives. In your holy Name, Amen.

Extension Activity

Who wants to put on a puppet show?! I thought so! Get creative with your puppets—make them out of socks or paper lunch bags, or use stuffed animals or action figures. In our family, we have two wacky puppets, Patricia and Patrick, who we bought at a bookstore—we'll get them in on the fun! Maybe you also own puppets you could use for your puppet show, or maybe you have a better idea that will work for your family. Great! Go with it!

Let's focus on self-control. Your puppets can exercise self-control in situations like these:

- Barbie takes Ken's favorite toy and breaks it.
- Mama Bear eats Daddy Bear's last ice cream treat from the freezer.
- Dragon teases Gnome about his outfit.
- Angel distracts Shepherd from his daily Bible reading.
- Any other conflict you can imagine between two characters that would test their self-control.

You may choose to write a script or just act out whatever comes to mind with your puppets. Maybe start out with the characters losing self-control. (Let's be honest—that sounds like it could be fun!) Then come up with a resolution so that they solve the problem in a way that demonstrates self-control.

As you act these scenarios out, try to apply them to your own life. Think about ways God is teaching you to use self-control, and ask Him to help you exhibit it in as many situations as you can.

Self-Control

Run toward the things that
bring you closer to God.

Scripture

"Do you not know that in a race all the runners run, but only one gets the prize? Run in such a way as to get the prize. Everyone who competes in the games goes into strict training. They do it to get a crown that will not last, but we do it to get a crown that will last forever. Therefore, I do not run like someone running aimlessly; I do not fight like a boxer beating the air. No, I strike a blow to my body and make it my slave so that after I have preached to others, I myself will not be disqualified for the prize."

– 1 CORINTHIANS 9:24-27

Parents

Have you ever heard of the Stanford Marshmallow Experiment? If not, you'll read about it below in the Families Devotional, so why don't you take a quick sneak peek at that before you come back to this?

Go ahead; I'll wait right here for you.

You'll want to pick back up right here.

Hi again! Glad you're back. That's pretty interesting stuff, right? It makes me wonder which option four-year-old Amy would have opted for. (I feel like she may have still been working on her self-control back then and would have probably eaten that one marshmallow for the instant gratification. But I guess we'll never know...)

Fortunately, while it's always a work in progress, my self-control has improved since my preschool stages of *probably taking the first hypothetical marshmallow I was offered.* One of the successes in my life is that I trained for and completed an entire marathon. No, I didn't win. No, I didn't run the whole time (but I did run most of it, and speed-walked that one big hill). No, it wasn't pretty. No, my knees haven't been the same ever since. But as Paul describes in his reminder of self-control in the above Scripture, it was important that I followed strict training. I didn't run aimlessly but rather consulted and closely followed a professional plan that guided me step-by-step to prepare me for the 26.2-mile race day.

Paul's reminder of self-control in the above Scripture from 1 Corinthians reminds me that I need to be living my life in a way that is focused on running the race "in such a way as to get the prize." As a Christian, this means I should be seeking out things that bring me closer to God. In doing this, I can "get a crown that will last forever" in my heavenly home someday.

Families

Stanford Marshmallow Experiment: A long time ago, probably before your parents were even born, all the way back in the 1970s, there was an experiment called the Marshmallow Test. A very famous university, Stanford, tested four-year-old children. The test went like this:

1. The four-year-olds were offered a marshmallow to eat right away.
2. They were told they could choose *not* to eat the marshmallow right away and instead get *two* marshmallows after fifteen minutes.
3. If they chose to eat *that* one marshmallow, they couldn't get the two marshmallows later.

The experiment had some pretty interesting findings, like that the children who were able to wait did better in academic areas later in life. This reminds me of something that we learn in the Bible. Having self-control means that we can live our lives for God, even when we are tempted to do something we shouldn't. But when we live our lives according to how the Bible teaches us to, we can "get a crown that will last forever," which means we can go to Heaven someday to be with Jesus.

I want to make something clear: It's not a bad thing if you think you would take the marshmallow offered in the first place. (I actually think my four-year-old self probably would have.) What I do want to share is that this is a good reminder that sometimes things are tempting to us. If you are tempted by something in your life, remember to try to make the decision God would want you to. Self-control is something we can all practice and get better at. If you're not sure what choice to make, pray about it, read your Bible, or check with a parent, pastor, or church friend to make the wise choice.

Prayer

Lord God, help us to wake up each day and race toward you in this life. We ask for your guidance when we are making the choices we should to bring glory to you. Thank you for giving us self-control and help us to use it to bring us closer to you. In your name, Amen.

Extension Activity

It's time for the Marshmallow Games! These are just for fun, but while you play, remember what we shared today about the marshmallow experiment and think about how important self-control is in our lives.

- **Marshmallow Toothpick Towers:** How high can you build a structure using only mini marshmallows and toothpicks? Build your own to see whose is the tallest, or work together to build the tallest one as a family.
- **Marshmallow Friends:** Create a marshmallow character using marshmallows (regular-sized and mini), chocolate chips, candy pieces, pretzels... whatever food items you have. Then name your marshmallow character and describe his or her story. What does she like? Where does he live? Why are they shaped that way?
- **Marshmallow Toss:** Grab a couple of cups and a couple of marshmallows. One person throws the marshmallow, and the other one tries to catch it in the cup. Who can make the furthest catch?

Self-Control

Seek God's approval above all;
live faithfully, not for the praise of
others, but as a true servant of Christ.

Scripture

"Am I now trying to win the approval of human beings or of God? Or am I trying to please people? If I were still trying to please people, I would not be a servant of Christ."

– GALATIANS 1:10

Parents

As a child, I remember the authority figures in my life always telling me, "Practice makes perfect." Well, as a people pleaser (something I have tried very hard to work on—reread that Galatians verse above for my reasoning here), I did what I was told. I kept practicing the piano, or soccer, or gymnastics, or my academic subjects, or (fill in the blank with any other practicable activity), but to no avail: never did I become perfect at any of the things I practiced.

Thankfully, my parents and close friends never had an expectation for my perfection. It was a standard that well-intentioned teachers encouraged me to strive for, which I eventually placed on myself. It wasn't until I was much older—college-age, perhaps—that I clung to the Galatians verse above to remind myself that I didn't have to be perfect. I didn't have to focus on doing what other people told me to do if I was focusing on what God was asking me to do in my life.

Recently, I read a piece of advice that said something like, "Every time you make a mistake, you can use that as another opportunity to practice and improve." I'm glad to see that the "practice makes perfect" mantra has become more or less a thing of the past. As an educator and mom, I want the children in my life to know that making mistakes means they can learn from them and grow from them! (Yes, it's good to strive for improvement, but I now prefer to encourage a "practice makes progress" approach instead.)

Often, a people-pleasing mentality gets in the way of God's guidance for me in my life. Instead of "seeking the approval of human beings," I want God to help me with my self-control to serve Him so I can do what He wants me to, not necessarily what others do. Very importantly, I have now learned to redirect my goals in alignment with what God's purpose for me is.

Families

Imagine that your parents ask you to clean your room or do another chore you may not be happy to do. What is your immediate response? Do you ask, "Do I *have* to?" in a whiny voice? (Yes, my own children do that.)

Instead of complaining that you *have* to do something, I have a suggestion: Why not look at it as you *get* to do that thing? Then, think of a reason that you have that task as a privilege. Let's try it:

- I *get* to do the dishes (because I had food and my belly is fed).
- I *get* to clean my room (because I have a home and shelter to keep me safe).
- I *get* to brush my teeth (because I am keeping myself healthy).
- I *get* to wake up early for school (because I am learning and becoming smarter, using the intelligence God gave me).

This shift in thinking allows us to cultivate self-control over things in our lives that we might tend to resist. What great things might you get to do today?

Similarly, God will lead us to do things in our lives. When we see His guidance, we should look at it as we get to do His will for us.

Prayer

Heavenly Father, we are so thankful that you show us your will in our lives. May we strive to do the things you ask us so that we are seeking your approval. Help us to have self-control when we may not feel willing to do what you ask. Thank you for your guidance and presence as we navigate your will for our lives. In Jesus' name we pray, Amen.

Extension Activity

Today, let's play one game—or more!—to be aware and mindful of our self-control. Pick from one of the choices below. Or any board game that requires careful, thoughtful choices and movements will do!

1. **Simon Says:** In this game, "Simon" tells the rest of the players what to do. But the other players only do it if the leader starts by saying "Simon says [hop on one foot]." Those who do the action when the leader doesn't start by saying "Simon says" are out. The last player standing becomes the new Simon.
   Self-control connection: Try to have self-control by listening carefully to the leader giving the orders.
2. **Jenga:** Build the block tower and then take turns removing blocks from the base and adding them to the top. This can be done in a competitive fashion, where the person who knocks over the tower loses the game, or it can be done in a teamwork fashion, where the team works together to build it as tall as possible.
   Self-control connection: Use slow, controlled movements and focus to help build the tower, and avoid the dreaded topple!
3. **Wooden Marble Maze Labyrinth:** This is a classic option that you can purchase online if you don't have access to it. Use the dials to navigate the wooden platform and get the marble through the maze. Be careful and cautious, however, because one wrong move can cause the marble to go into a hole, and you'll have to restart!
   Self-control connection: Think ahead about what might happen with each move you make. Use controlled, careful movements to help guide the marble where you want it to go.

Self-Control

Master your thoughts, seek peace, and focus on what is true and noble.

Scripture

"Better a patient person than a warrior, one with self-control than one who takes a city."

– PROVERBS 16:32

"We take captive every thought and make it obedient to Christ."

– 2 CORINTHIANS 10:5

"Finally, brothers and sisters, whatever is true, whatever is noble, whatever is right, whatever is pure, whatever is lovely, whatever is admirable—if anything is excellent or praiseworthy—think about such things."

– PHILIPPIANS 4-8

Parents

In my family, the show, *Mr. Rogers' Neighborhood,* was a staple. Henrietta Pussycat, Daniel Tiger, and King Friday the VIII puppets paraded around our living room, as they enacted the story of our make-believe games after spending time in the calming, nurturing world we entered through our TV set.

Countless times, my parents took us to the TV set to meet Mr. McFeely and get an Eat 'n Park cookie (if you are from Western PA, you know how much of a treat this would be!), as Sundays were family days at WQED. This was much to my grandpa's dismay, a Presbyterian minister who, although he loved Mr. Rogers, did not love us missing church for this event. He even wrote a letter to Fred Rogers to express his concern, and in his typical fashion, Mr. Rogers returned his letter voicing his apology over the situation!

I always thought Mr. Rogers was admirable growing up, but it wasn't until I began teaching that I really grew to appreciate him. I started reading every book/biography about his life and grew to realize how ahead of his time he was in the field of early childhood education and social-emotional learning. His heart behind what he did so greatly resonated with my prayer in working with children, and I learned, and am still learning, so much from him. Not only that, but I also grew to greatly admire his character and discipline behind the scenes, which, I believe, contributed to him being so faithful, consistent, and impactful.

His morning routine consisted of swimming laps each day and going through his prayer list—praying by name for each person written down. He spent a lot of time in solitude and with the Lord. He was a man of great self-discipline.

So, when thinking of self-discipline, next to Jesus, one of my biggest role models is Mr. Rogers! What I appreciated about him was that when it came to self-discipline with our feelings and thoughts, he didn't think we should sweep them under the rug, push them away, and ignore them. Rather, he once said that, "Anything that's human is mentionable, and anything that is mentionable can be more manageable." He also once said that "Human beings are not born with self-control. We have to learn what to do with the 'mad' that we feel. Learning to control ourselves is a long, hard process. It happens little by little."

Sometimes, as a child and even recently, I used to think that some feelings were bad. Happiness and joy were okay, but anger and sadness were not. I don't know exactly why I thought that, but I always felt pressure to turn my thoughts and feelings around rather than really sorting through the hurt or pain I was experiencing. However, now teaching children and having two of my own, all coming with **big**, real feelings, I have realized how detrimental that is. It is so important to allow them to have space to explore what they're feeling and know they are loved in it and through it as they learn how to handle those **big** emotions.

I think the biggest battleground we sometimes face can be in our own minds and souls. Our thoughts and feelings, without self-discipline or groundedness in God, can so easily rule us. I remember going through the loss of a grandparent and having so many big feelings—unlike anything I had ever experienced: grief, sadness, anger, confusion, etc. It was so hard, and being in my 20s, it was my first real loss.

I distinctly remember my sister-in-law texting me the verses above from 2 Corinthians and Philippians (looking back now, I know God spoke through her), and they were so helpful. God wasn't saying to ignore what I felt, but rather, take what I felt to him. After laying it all out to God and meditating on those words (and through a lot of prayer and time), I felt God transforming my feelings and thoughts. Yes, I was still grieving that loss, but I felt Him transform my thoughts and feelings, and I felt His presence in the midst of the pain.

Self-control over our thoughts and emotions is a daily, hourly, even minute-by-minute surrender! My brain can go down a dark rabbit hole if I do not spend time with the Lord and constantly go back to Him. I think Mr. Rogers and these verses embody that self-control is a discipline; a constant choice to lay ourselves and what we feel down at His feet and allow Him to have control over it all. In turn, we need to give the sweet little people entrusted to us love, space, patience, and grace as they learn to navigate what they think and feel, letting them know that it's okay and that we're here. As we surrender our feelings to Christ with humility and authenticity, hopefully, we can show our kids that He is big enough (more than enough!) to handle the big things they feel.

Families

Read the lyrics that follow from the song "What Do You Do with the Mad that You Feel?" written by Mr. Rogers (you may also be able to find the song on YouTube!):

What do you do with the mad that you feel
When you feel so mad you could bite?
When the whole wide world seems oh, so wrong...
And nothing you do seems very right?

What do you do? Do you punch a bag?
Do you pound some clay or some dough?
Do you round up friends for a game of tag?
Or see how fast you go?

It's great to be able to stop
When you've planned a thing that's wrong,
And be able to do something else instead
And think this song:

I can stop when I want to
Can stop when I wish
I can stop, stop, stop any time.
And what a good feeling to feel like this
And know that the feeling is really mine.
Know that there's something deep inside
That helps us become what we can.
For a girl can be someday a woman
And a boy can be someday a man.

(Lyrics courtesy: THE NEIGHBORHOOD ARCHIVE - All Things Mister Rogers)

Sometimes we feel joy, and happiness, and excitement! However, other times we feel mad, angry, and upset. Think about a time that you felt mad or sad. What did you do that helped you?

It is okay to feel that mad! God created us with hearts and minds that were meant to feel and think. However, it is important that we respond to those thoughts and feelings in a way that is helpful, healthy, and honors Him.

God wants to help us when we feel hurt, and He is big enough to hold it all, even when we sometimes feel like we could explode! He is always there to listen and wants us to go to Him with our cares and concerns.

Talk about, as a family, some things you can do if you're upset! What might help you sort through the *mad* that you feel?

Prayer

God, thank you for the assurance that we can come to you with all of our feelings, big and small, hard and easy, and that you love us through it all. Thank you for being big enough to hold it all. Please take captive any thought displeasing to you, and replace it with what is true, admirable, and worthy of praise. We love you, Lord. In Jesus' name, Amen.

Extension Activity

Create in your house a little calm-down corner (or calm zone!) to go to if you feel upset or need some quiet time with God. Put inside some favorite stuffed animals, calming music (or favorite worship music!) to listen to, Play-Doh or putty to hold, crayons and paper to color, blocks to build with, encouraging Scripture verses, etc. Anytime you feel sad or mad or upset, go to this corner, take a deep breath, and spend some time with God. Allow Him to help you sort through your feelings and thoughts! (This is good for parents, too!)

Self-Control

Nothing is impossible
with God.

Scripture

"Jesus looked at them and said, 'With man this is impossible, but with God all things are possible.'"

– MATTHEW 19:26

Parents

I perform in two improv groups. I do love performing scripted plays, but for some reason, improv has resonated with me in a lot of ways. I think it's the fact that we are given something random to work with, and we have to turn it into something interesting or funny. (Thankfully, my years of quick wit and sarcastic tendencies serve me well in an improv setting.) One thing that intimidates most actors about improv is the unknown: many of my very talented theatrical friends refuse to try improv because they don't like performing what they don't know and can't plan for.

But in life, that's the reality, isn't it? We can't know what is going to happen to us. We can't plan for those things because, like I said, we don't know what is coming our way.

Life is unplanned. (I'm guessing you are a parent or guardian figure, and you are very unsurprised by that statement.) But sometimes, we get into our own flow, our plans, our day-to-day routines, and things seem to be going just as planned. Woohoo! We're doing great and are in control of our lives! (You probably see where I'm going with this, don't you?) Then, BAM! Something happens to throw us off, and we realize: we are not really in control at all, are we?

But we can control how we respond in these situations. As the Scripture above says, God makes all things possible, even when those things don't align with our own plans. So we can pray for His guidance when the unexpected comes up and follow His guidance through the unknowns. Having prayerful self-control when things go awry allows us to follow God's plan for us, because He makes all things possible!

Families

I love Mondays! Now, you may hear a lot of people say they get a "case of the Mondays" or that they really don't like Mondays. In fact, when I share with people that I love Mondays, they often look at me like I have two heads (which I don't, I promise)!

Maybe you can even relate to those people who say they don't like Mondays. If you're school age, maybe you dislike getting up early and having to be at school after a fun, relaxing weekend. Maybe you just don't like the schedule and routine. Maybe you've picked up a dislike for Mondays because of the adults in your life with that same attitude.

But to me, a Monday is a fresh slate! It is a chance to start a brand-new week. It is an opportunity to plan for what you can and to await the new adventures that are sure to come your way. In fact, my ten-year-old daughter is similar to me. She is a planner. She squealed excitedly when we went into the student planner section when we recently went back-to-school shopping. She loves writing down her schedule and the upcoming plans she has, using fun markers and stickers. (Her artistic ability is unreal—she is actually our illustrator for this book!) She loves tackling each week—and the new year—with a fresh start!

As much as we can write down our plans, many times we won't know what is coming our way. Sure, we can write down our activities and schedules, and it's good to be prepared when we can be. But when life comes our way, we will often find that things happen that don't match up with what we've planned: A storm may come to delay the big game. A friend might be upset with us, and we don't know why. We might come down with an unexpected case of the flu. But even when things don't go as planned, we can ask God for His help in navigating the unknowns. God can make anything possible, even when things don't go along with our plans. We can pray to ask God for self-control to follow what He wants us to do when unplanned things happen.

Prayer

Heavenly Father, you are the author of the story of our life. You know exactly what will happen, even when unknown things come our way. Help us to ask you for your guidance when things happen that are unplanned. We are so thankful that you go before us in every circumstance, and we pray that you help us follow you as we navigate everything in our lives. In your holy name we pray, Amen.

Extension Activity

We are going to play a few of my favorite improv games! Just like life is often unplanned, improv allows you to take brand-new ideas and make things up as you go.

GAME 1—Alphabet: Take turns saying sentences that tell a story. Not too tricky, right? Except that each person has to use the next letter of the alphabet. So, for instance, if Person One says, "Apples are falling from the sky!"

Person Two might say, "But none of them have hit my head—yet!"

And Person Three could continue with, "Could we try to make some apple pie with them?"

Then the next person's sentence would start with the letter D, and so on. Go back to person one once all players have taken a turn. Try to make it the whole way through the story without missing a letter of the alphabet at the start of each sentence—and to add an extra challenge, pick a random letter partway through the alphabet to start your story, and go through until you get back to it!

GAME 2—Numbers: Give each other a certain number from one to ten. Then tell a story or make up a scene, but each player must only use their number of words in each of their sentences. So if a group had 1, 4, 7, and 10 words, a story might go something like this: (Person with four words) "Do you like cheese?" (Person with 10 words) "I do like cheese a bit but actually prefer yogurt." (Person with one word) "Ew!" (Person with seven words) "Could I try some of your yogurt?" And so on. Alternate so each person gets a few turns, and try to keep the story on track using your number of words.

About the Authors

Alexandra Schroder is a mom, kindergarten teacher, and lover of Jesus. Living with her husband, two kids, and exuberant Goldendoodle, she feels grateful to raise her family in the same special small town in Pennsylvania in which she grew up. In addition to experiencing wonder, joy, and curiosity through the eyes of the little humans in her life, Alex loves running, traveling with her family, and good conversations with friends over coffee. This is her first book.

Amy Winner is married to her best friend, Dr. Andrew Winner, and they have two amazing children, Aila and Archie. They have also recently welcomed a new addition to their family: the cutest puppy, Oscar! Amy has been an elementary educator for almost two decades. She is deeply involved in her local arts community, often sharing the stage with her children. She's also a fan of all things Disney! Amy considers it one of her greatest blessings from her Lord and Savior Jesus Christ, to co-author Cute Fruit with her amazing sister-in-law, Alex, and hopes many families experience the mutual love of faith, family, and fun through this devotional.

THANK YOU FOR READING OUR BOOK!

DOWNLOAD YOUR FREE GIFTS

Just to say thanks for buying and reading our book,
we would like to give you a few free bonus gifts,
no strings attached!

Scan the QR Code:

We appreciate your interest in our book and value your feedback as it helps us improve future versions.
We would appreciate it if you could leave your invaluable review on Amazon.com with your feedback.
Thank you!

www.ingramcontent.com/pod-product-compliance
Lightning Source LLC
Chambersburg PA
CBHW070539090426
42735CB00013B/3023
* 9 7 9 8 9 0 1 5 8 0 0 3 5 *